CHILDREN'S MUSEUM OF PITTSBURGH

TOUGH ART

Making Art as Strong as Kids

TABLE OF CONTENTS

FOREWORD

Lucky the child who meets an artist, luckier still are those who see an artist at work. For starters, artists tend to be more adventurous than parents—which is a good thing. In fact, as a group, artists are driven by an uncompromising desire for self-expression. The better of them convince the world through their art to see differently, to revise current notions of beauty in favor of other, newer ones to be found in the artist's work. Thus, artists are reformers and indispensable to societal change. The prosaic among us call them "problem solvers," but I find that designation too pragmatic. Artists of any media demonstrate the power of imagination. It's just there that artists and many children become somewhat concentric, recalling the old saying that all children are artists until age six, seven, eight, nine, etc. Children want to self-express too, until they don't.

The Children's Museum's fifteen-year-old project of sponsoring artists to enjoy a residency is aptly called "Tough Art," since making good art is quite difficult. It forces a marriage of inspiration and skill few adults can manage. About seventy artists have now participated in the "Tough Art" residency, many

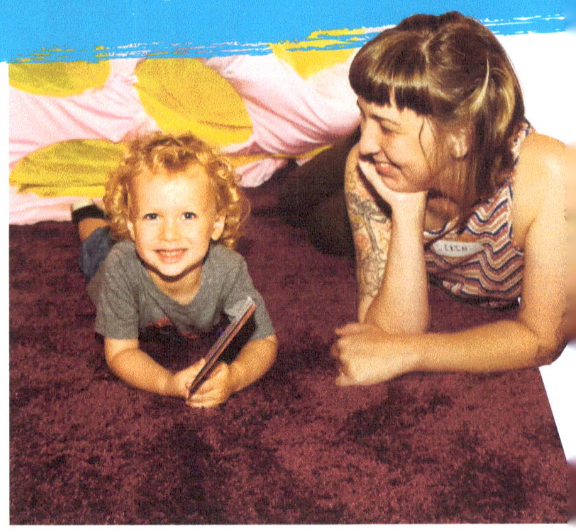

of them leaving behind something for the Museum's art collection—an accretion of past ambitions and happy alliances between artists and children. The relationship is mutually beneficial, most artists receptive to the perceptions and working methods of their young counterparts. The Museum staff benefits as well, observing ways of creating and collaborating that are frequently inspiring. Tough Art has a national reputation, as does the Museum itself as it is so widely cited as one of the best in the country. Jane Werner's leadership deserves such attention and Pittsburgh deserves credit for its sustained support of the Museum.

One of the Children's Museum's most praiseworthy achievements relates directly to the city. The institution has been the catalyst, savior, and adaptor of the old Allegheny Post Office, the abandoned but splendid Buhl

The relationship is mutually beneficial, most artists receptive to the perceptions and working methods of their young counterparts.

Planetarium, the magisterial nearby Carnegie Library, and most recently, the successful redesign of adjacent properties into one of the city's most popular squares. In helping save the Northside, the Museum has helped both Pittsburghers and hundreds of thousands of out-of-town visitors see again the city's memorable, if sometimes tattered, architecture.

Working beside artists in a distinguished physical environment is a fortunate opportunity for the young. Visual creativity offers them a lifetime of joy.

Richard Armstrong
Director, The Solomon R. Guggenheim Museum and Foundation

4: *Urchin Searchin Sound*
   (Arvid Tomayko and H.Gene Thompson, 2017)
5: *Fist Sized Survival* (Nobi Nagasawa, 2016)

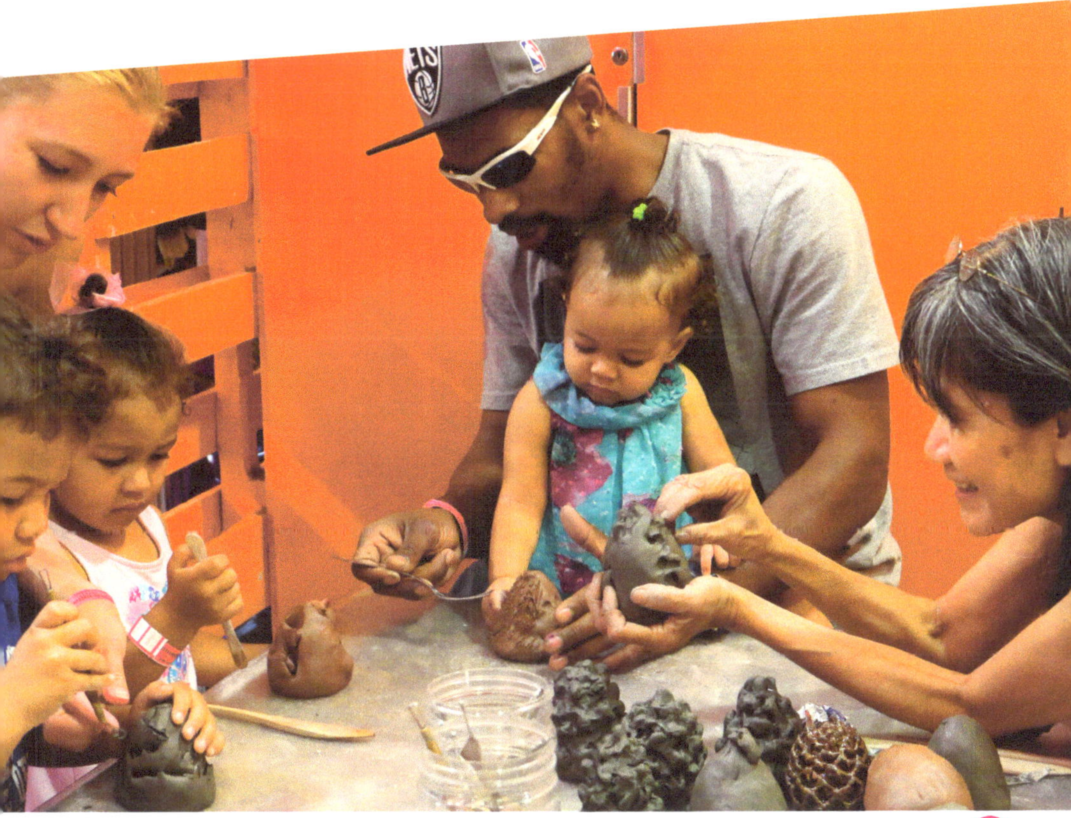

INTRODUCTION

In 2006, I was sitting in a window seat coming back from California

after visiting my friend Ned Kahn, an artist I've known and admired for over thirty-five years. We'd had a wonderful time looking at his new work, talking about a commission he was doing for our museum, and playing with a few things he was working on in his shop. I was thinking about where to find the next "Ned Kahn," an artist who could make people think differently about their worlds using the most robust of materials.

Though we'd had many artists in the Children's Museum of Pittsburgh over the years, the vast majority were crushed when their delicate pieces of art were unexpectedly transformed by our young visitors in unforeseen (albeit amazing) ways. The artists would leave with broken pieces of wood, bent metal, and paint chips—their notions of both art and children in shreds.

My mind wandered thinking about the work Ned had been doing for years for people across nations. The work not only held up to the robust play of children and adults but helped them think differently, discover new ways of seeing, and made them curious about the world. My thoughts also drifted to a conversation I had at the Museum with artist Keny Marshall, who was interested in focusing more of our attention on artists.

And there, somewhere over Kansas, the idea of Tough Art hatched.

What would happen if we gave artists money, time, and access to people like Ned and our audience? What would happen if artists worked alongside our amazing staff in one of the most challenging public space environments, a children's museum? What would happen if we gave artists the opportunity to think differently about what it means to make art in different environments? And most importantly, what would happen if artists took children seriously and worked to see the world from their perspective?

We started small, with a few graduate students from Carnegie Mellon University's MFA program, and it was a success. We loved not only the works they produced but the energy they brought to the Museum. So we continued.

Fifteen years later, over seventy artists have been embedded in the Museum for a Tough Art residency. Not all Tough Artists have been successful, but we think that disappointment is part of the process of making art.

art in a new way. It shakes up their notions of art to experience a sheep spaceship or hear steps speak or see a roller coaster robot for plants.

What would happen if artists took children seriously and worked to see the world from their perspective?

The Tough Art Program has made us think differently, too. It energizes the Museum space like no other program. The artists are always interesting and creative, sometimes frustrated, and most times happy to be among the wonderful folks we get to work with every day. Most importantly, it gets our visitors to view

Tough Art is essential to the Children's Museum's mission *to provide innovative and inclusive museum experiences that inspire kindness, joy, creativity, and curiosity for all learners.* Through Tough Art, we are practicing what most successful artists and children do naturally. We are questioning our own model of the world.

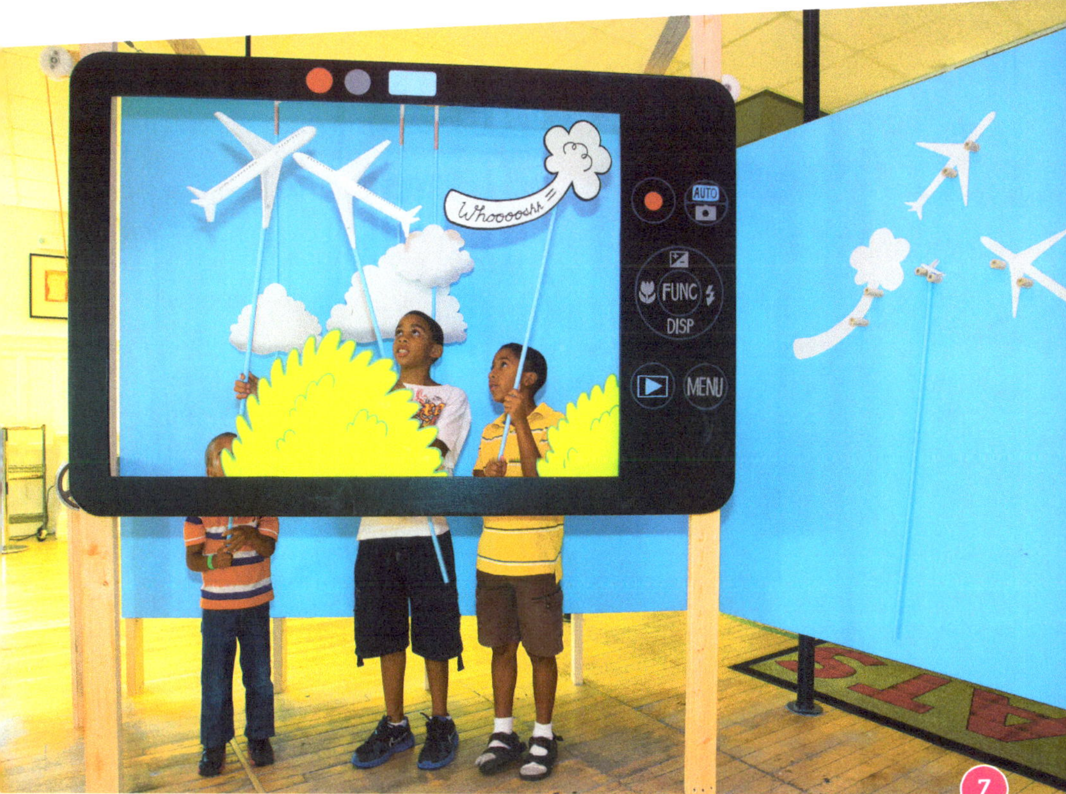

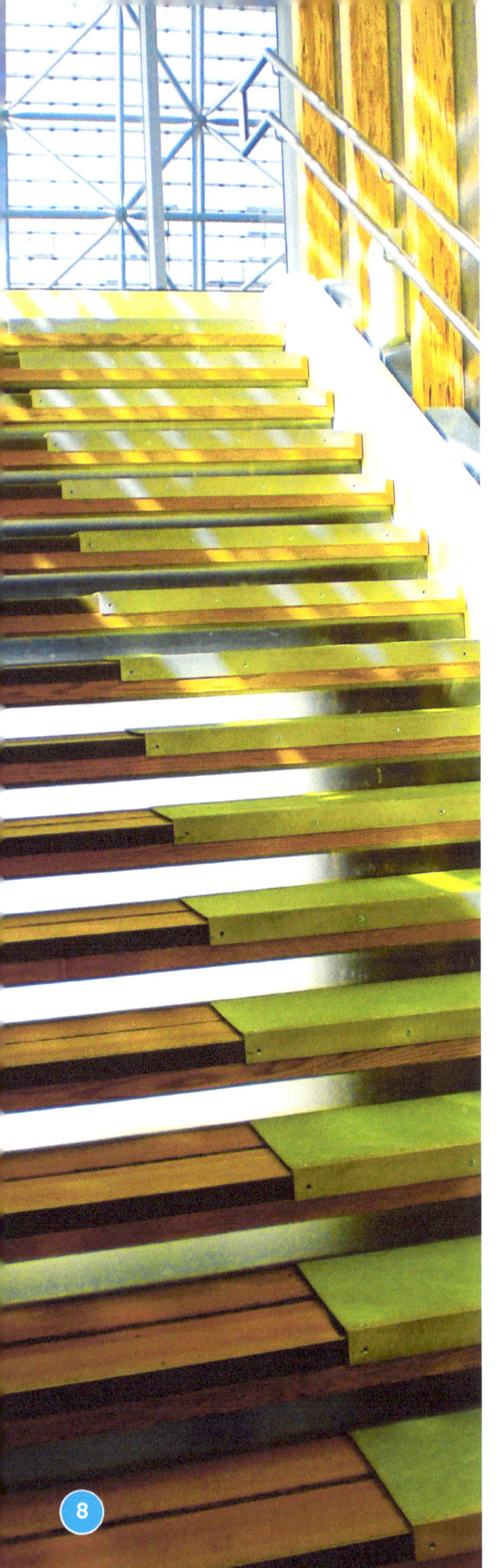

Acknowledgments

This book celebrates the Tough Art program and some of the unique experiences these artworks have provided audiences over the past fifteen years. While it was not possible to include every work, many of which cannot be adequately captured in photos and words, we hope our photographs and accounts will provide a representative sample of the sensations and joys that stem from these residencies and the artists.

This book is also intended to provide other museum professionals with insights and know-how for creating similar residencies or partnerships with artists in their own institutions. It is further aimed at artists who want to know more about working with hands-on museums or creating public art. As we document some of what has made this program so valuable and exciting to us, we hope to inspire others to innovate in their own practices.

There are many people over fifteen years that have been instrumental to making Tough Art possible. Our thanks to the Children's Museum of Pittsburgh's Board and staff, past and present, who played a crucial role in Tough Art's development.

The first few years of Tough Art were made possible through funding from the Institute of Museum and Library Services, Snee-Reinhardt Charitable Foundation, Fine Foundation, and Winchester Thurston School.

Lacey Murray, our Tough Art Manager, has overseen all activities for the residency for the past six years and assisted with the production of this book. Greg Russo, Greg Witt, Candice Fischer, and Toby Fraley provide technical assistance, budgeting support and mentoring to the Tough Artists throughout their process. Tough Art's success is due to their commitment to the process.

Our thanks extend to former employees who nurtured the program through the beginning years. Chris Siefert, Keny Marshall, and Penny Lodge all played key roles in the creation and development of the program. They were supported by Lisa Carvajal, Nicholas Hohman, Kristopher Kaminsky, PJ Zimmerlink, Lisa Brahms, and Matt Tuite. This program would not exist without their care.

Special thanks to the friends, supporters and mentors of the program including Ned Kahn, artist extraordinaire and inspiration for the program. We are additionally grateful to Ned for producing an afterword for this book. The late Tom Sokolowski, former Director of the Warhol, was a champion of the program from the start acting as a mentor, critic, and advisor. We all miss his insights and his crazy, idea-filled phone calls. Our thanks also to Richard Armstrong for the wonderful foreword to this book.

Thanks also to Jedd Hakimi of Point Line Projects for helping guide this book's production and to Scott Sosebee of Sosebee Design for the book's design.

Claire Pillsbury deserves special recognition for her many roles in this program including being a guest mentor and curator. Most importantly, she is the co-writer of this book. Thank you, Claire, for your unwavering support.

Anne Fullenkamp, our Senior Director of the Center for Creative Experiences, is the hero of this story. She is the other co-writer of this book, acting as both the bridge between the past and the future. Her creativity, perseverance, and work ethic have made this book a reality. We are so very grateful.

And finally, thank you to the artists, visitors, and children who have spent time at the Children's Museum of Pittsburgh.

You've all made us all think differently about the world.

Jane Werner
*Executive Director of the
Children's Museum of Pittsburgh*

7: *Things That Fly* (John Peña, 2012)
8: *Temperamental Stairs*
   (Agnes Bolt and Arthur Jones, 2010)

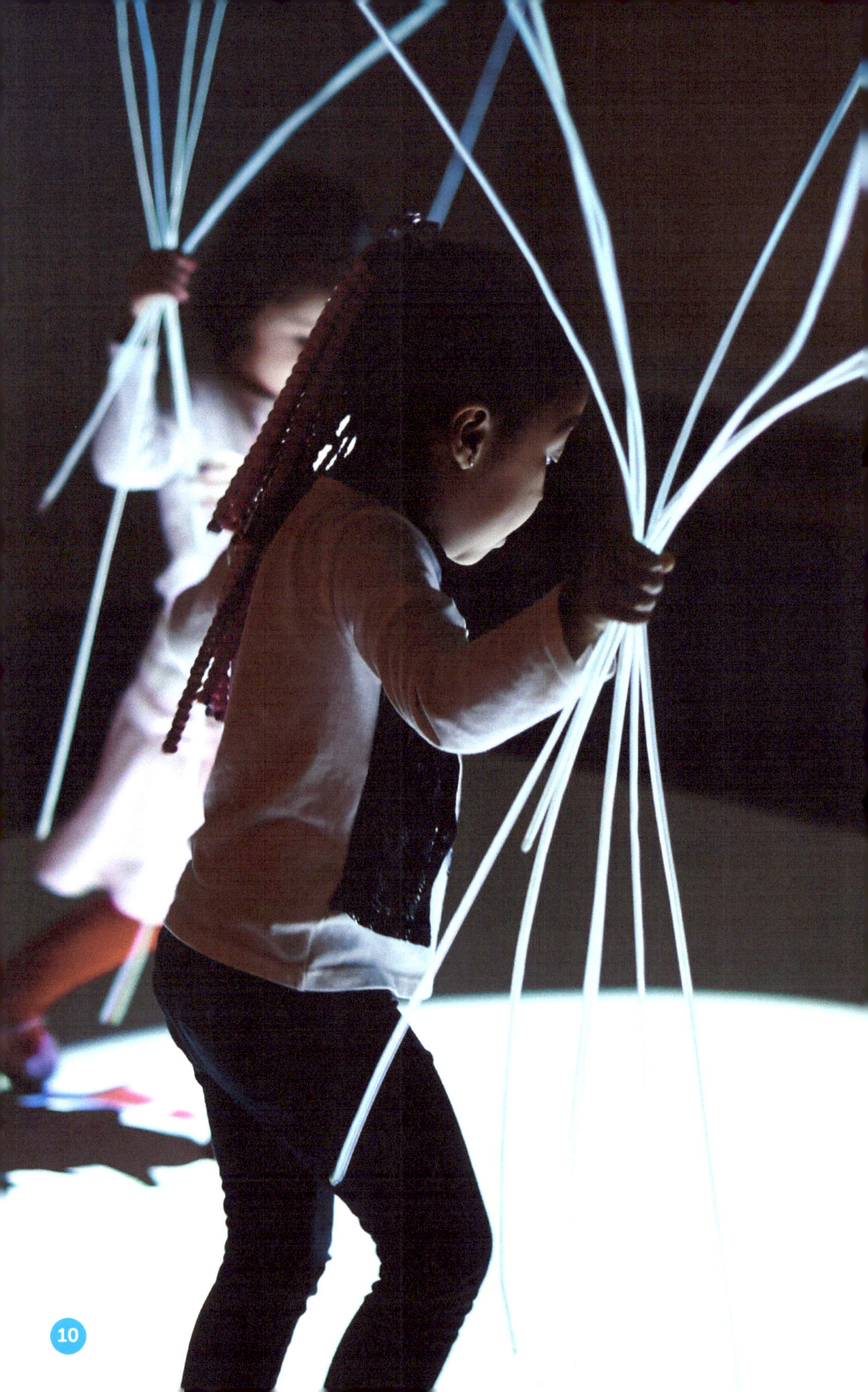

WHAT IS TOUGH ART?

The term "tough art" may initially strike some as paradoxical—

especially in the context of a museum. Art housed in museums is often set behind velvet ropes, moisture-controlled, carefully watched over, and, above all, not to be touched. This art experience perpetuates the idea that all great art is delicate and meant mostly for the eyes.

The collision of strength and beauty in the official name of our artist residency—Tough Art—is in many ways tailored to a children's museum. Children don't just experience with their eyes; they experience with as many senses as they can muster. Everything that can be climbed on, swung from, slid down, flipped over, and banged on will be in the service of play and exploration. Bringing original art into a children's museum means producing work that will intrigue young visitors' curious minds, while standing up to their equally inquisitive bodies.

Since 2007, each summer the Children's Museum of Pittsburgh has invited four individual and/or teams of emerging artists to participate in a museum residency during which they develop a new work to be exhibited in the Museum and, if tough enough, may be added to its permanent collection. One of our chief goals is to create a piece that will engage young minds and stand up to young bodies for as long as possible. But anything that beckons children to engage must be prepared for the prying fingers of experimentation.

In this context, making art *tough* is quite literal—making a piece robust enough for eager, unexpected, and improvised interactions. The materials, construction, and potential usages must all be thoughtfully considered, tested, and reworked for durability, to create a rewarding experience

Origins

The idea for Tough Art can be traced back to the Museum's large-scale renovation in 2004, a moment which provided an opportunity to take stock of the Museum's priorities. Part of this process entailed collaborating with several experimental artists, who

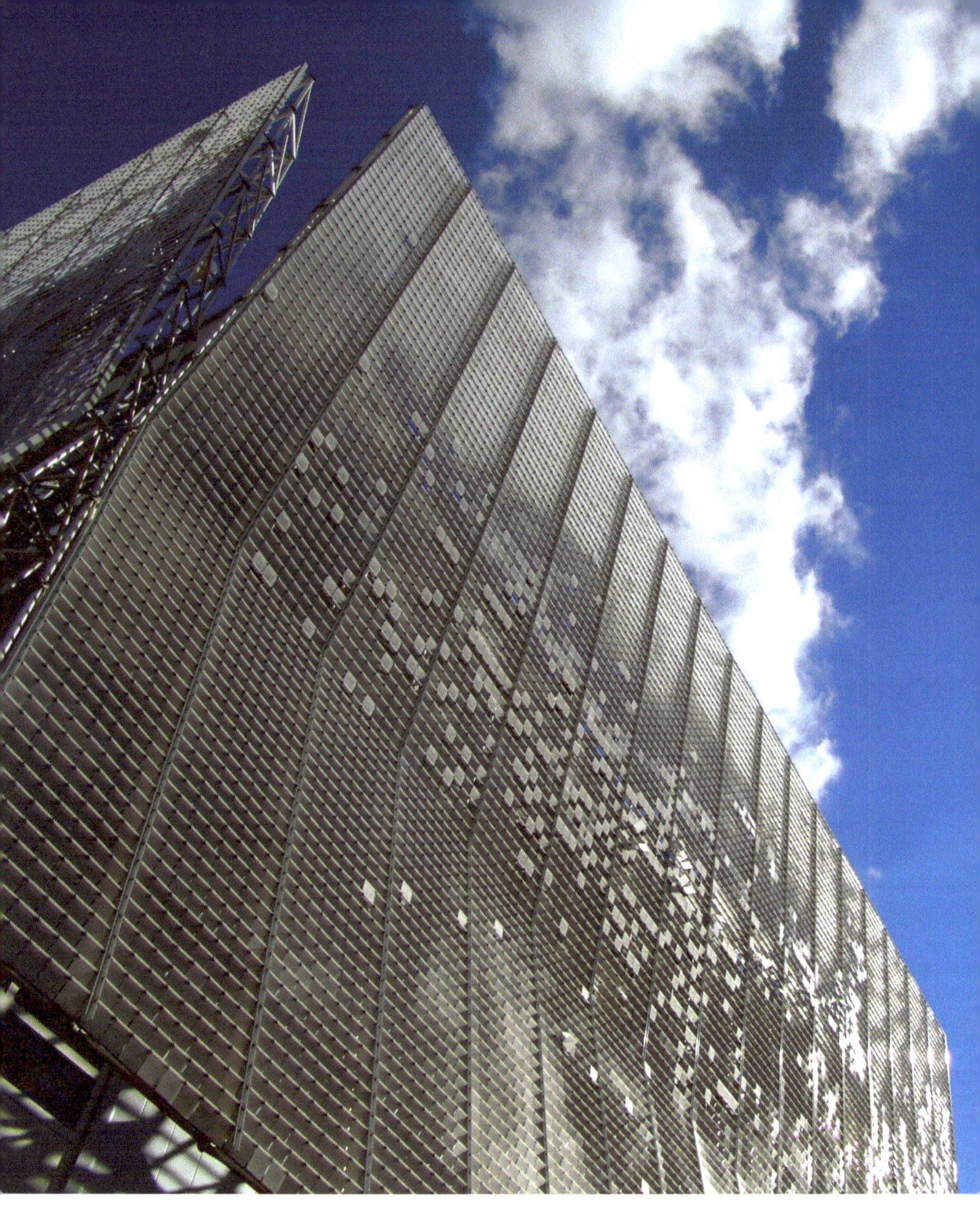

contributed to the transformation. Ned Kahn clad the center building with thousands of wind-responsive, translucent shingles; Dick Esterle hung a hypnotizing array of pink and fuchsia ribbons—each several stories tall—inside the Museum's magnificent, domed atrium; and Elizabeth and Chris Siefert produced three fifteen-foot-long, rotating fiberglass fish, which float above the parking lot propped up on twenty-foot metal poles. The success of these collaborations fueled the ambition to continue working with contemporary artists, few of whom typically have experience creating specifically for children.

Artist and former Exhibit Designer Keny Marshall pointed out that any motivated artist could create work for children—or *toughen* up their art—with a few basic ingredients: 1) materials; 2) space; 3) guidance; and 4) compensation. In short, a recipe for a residency through which artists could make use of the Museum's resources and expertise to create a new piece of Tough Art.

But what do artists get out of creating works for children? And, more importantly, why do children need art?

Innovation that Inspires

Most kids don't bother differentiating between an *art* object and a *play* object. If given the opportunity, they would just as likely swing from a giant Calder mobile as they would a set of monkey bars. Why, then, is it so important to bring art and emerging artists into the Museum?

Some of the reasons are embedded in the Museum's mission statement:

> *To provide innovative and inclusive museum experiences that inspire kindness, joy, creativity, and curiosity for all learners.*

There are plenty of experiences and objects we already know kids will love, and there is a great deal to appreciate about dinosaurs, trains, and robots. The challenge we gave ourselves with Tough Art is making something completely novel that will *inspire kindness, joy, creativity, and curiosity*. We are after objects, sensations, ideas, and experiences that will inspire kids even on their initial encounter. Providing wholly unfamiliar yet inspiring experiences for children—and their families—requires genuine *innovation*. And emerging artists are perhaps more suited than anyone to imagine an experience that has never before existed.

For emerging artists working in experimental media who are used to fringe audiences and boutique galleries, it may never even occur to them to consider children part of their audience. Yet those of us working in children's museums know there is a huge demographic eager and willing to jump headfirst

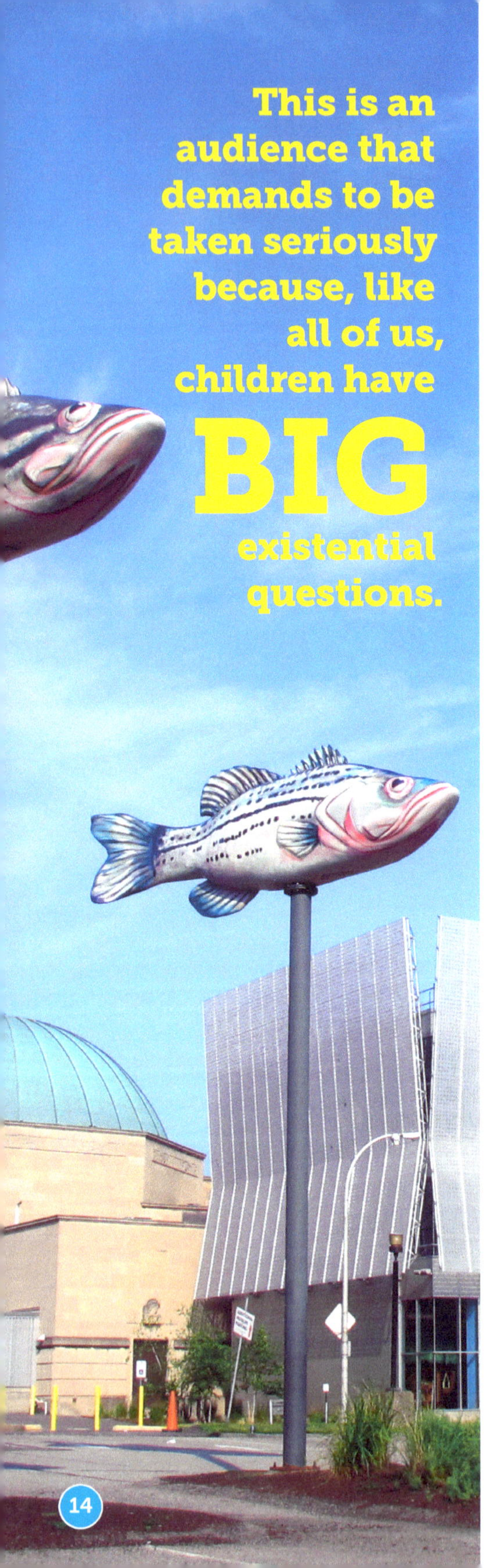

into new experiences, both literally and figuratively. This is an audience that demands to be taken seriously because, like all of us, children have big existential questions. Artists and their art can inspire kids with ways to address those questions.

In our experience, the benefit of bringing together emerging artists and children is a two-way street. Innovative artwork can spark children to think in new ways and imagine futures that would never have existed otherwise. Likewise, as artists become more acquainted with the unique joys and possibilities of creating artworks for family audiences, they see their practice expanding in unexpected ways. Creating art with constraints can often be generative. In fact, a number of Tough Artists continue their artistic practice with young audiences in mind, and a few Tough Artists have even come to work full time at the Museum after their residencies.

The Tough Artists' impact on the Museum begins with the children but extends in all directions. Exhibits Director Greg Russo has pointed out the unique benefits inherent in Museum staff engaging with a rotating group of emerging artists and their varying specialties. "Working with new people from different backgrounds, using different media," he explains, "helps to keep [the Museum staff's] own perspective from growing stale." Innovation and inspiration require constant renewal, and both can be fueled by new perspectives, whether

As with all good art and experimentation, not everything has worked out as planned. . . .

those come from the emerging artists or their young audiences as they first encounter the art.

As with all good art and experimentation, not everything has worked out as planned, but the program has proved tough in its own right as it has adapted and evolved over the years. This willingness to change in response to feedback is, in fact, the most defining feature of

Tough Art. Prototyping—a process of envisioning, experimenting, testing, and responding—is crucial to how this residency survives, and it may also be the single most important component to building a tough artwork.

David Butts

GIANT

Ceding Control

David came to Tough Art having recently retired from a thirty-year career as an architect and looking to jumpstart his next career as a full-time artist.

As the first out-of-town artist we hosted (visiting from Portland, Oregon), David had no other connections to Pittsburgh, so he was 100% focused on the Tough Art residency. This created extra time to experiment with his idea, construct his prototype, and even work with the staff on non-Tough Art projects.

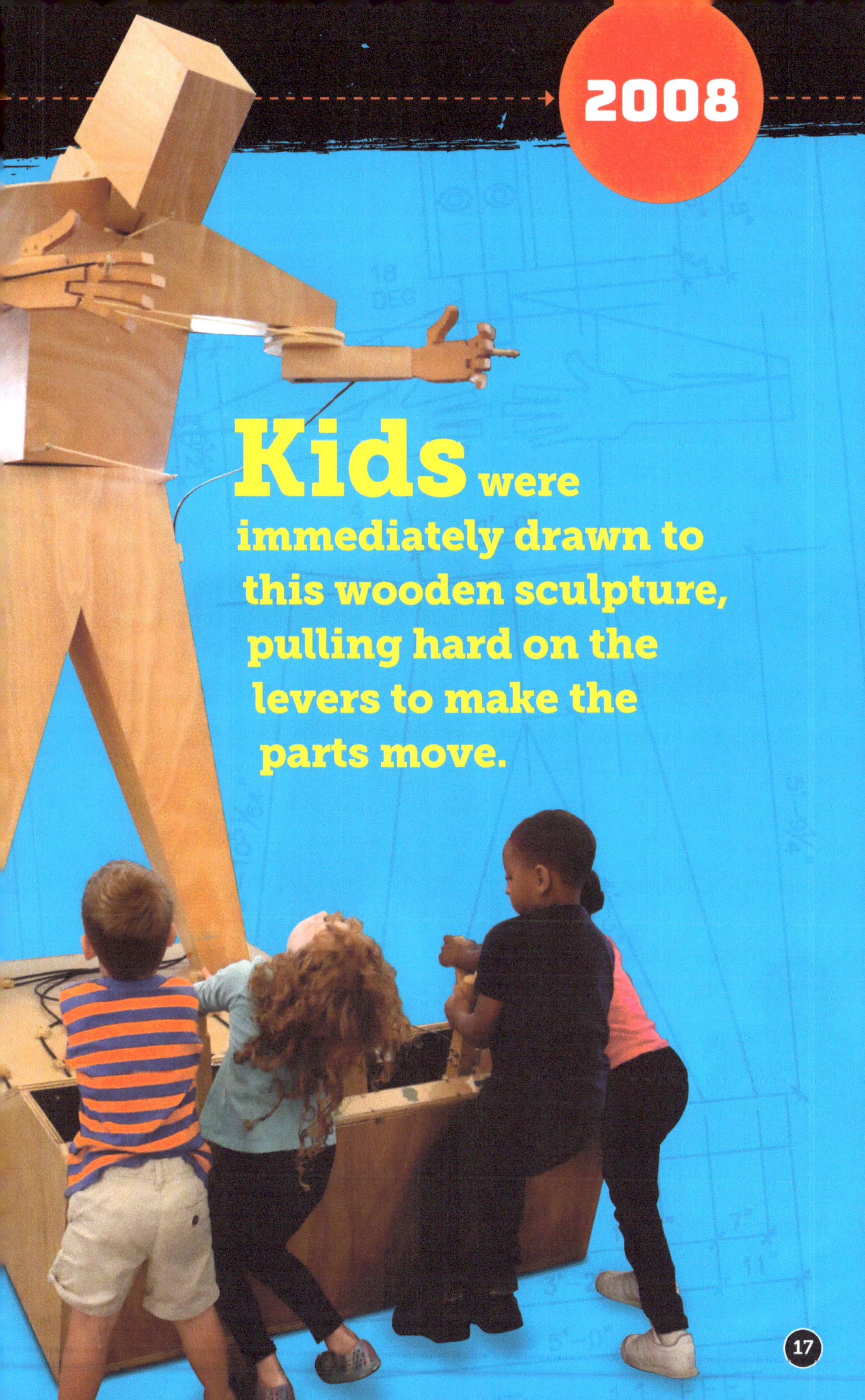

Kids were immediately drawn to this wooden sculpture, pulling hard on the levers to make the parts move.

David had an ambitious idea from the start. He observed that children are often physically controlled by adults—picked up and carried, strapped into strollers and seats—and he wanted to reverse the dynamic by building a giant man that small children could physically control and manipulate. He made detailed architectural-style drawings and spent time observing how kids play. He also prototyped *a lot*, building multiple maquettes of his idea, including one where the head had a fully articulated face. He designed a variety of levers that would allow users to alter the head's facial expressions by raising an eyebrow or winking an eye.

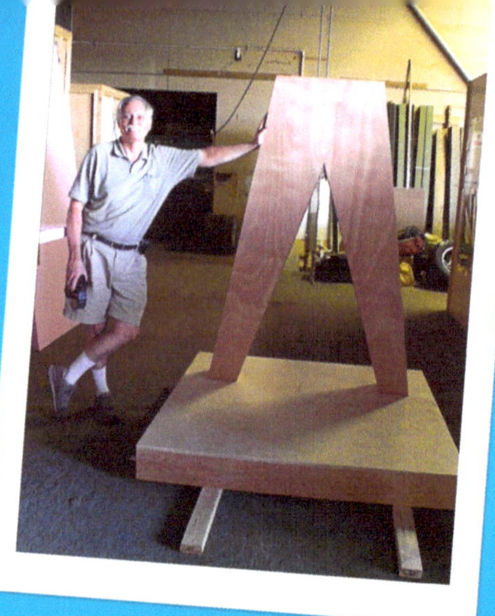

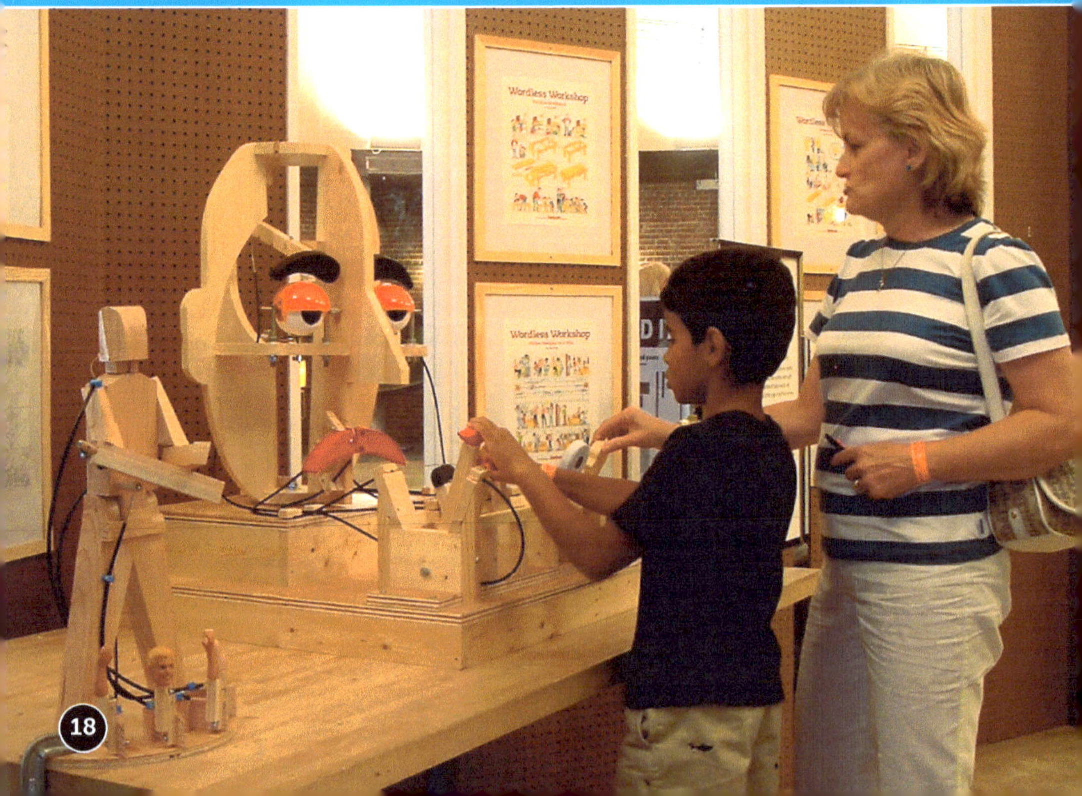

IN REST POSITION, EYES CLOSED, ARMS FOLDED.

FABRIC SHIRT

14'-0"

RIGHT ARM

HEAD

TORSO

LEFT ARM

BASE AND LEGS FIXED
PLYWOOD - HARD TO CLIMB

HEAD, ARMS, HANDS & TORSO -
PAPER MACHÉ ON WIRE FRAME

HEAD TIPS FORWARD, EYES OPEN

TORSO LEANS FORWARD

ARMS SWING OUT

LEVERS PULL CABLES - OPERATE FIGURE

4'-2" TYPICAL 8-YEAR OLD

8'-0"

SHOCK ABSORBER DAMPENS & SLOWS MOTION

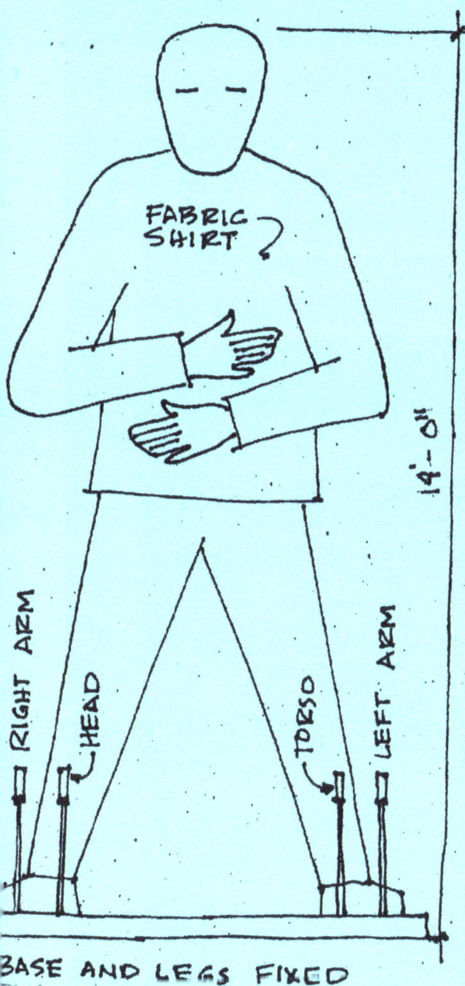

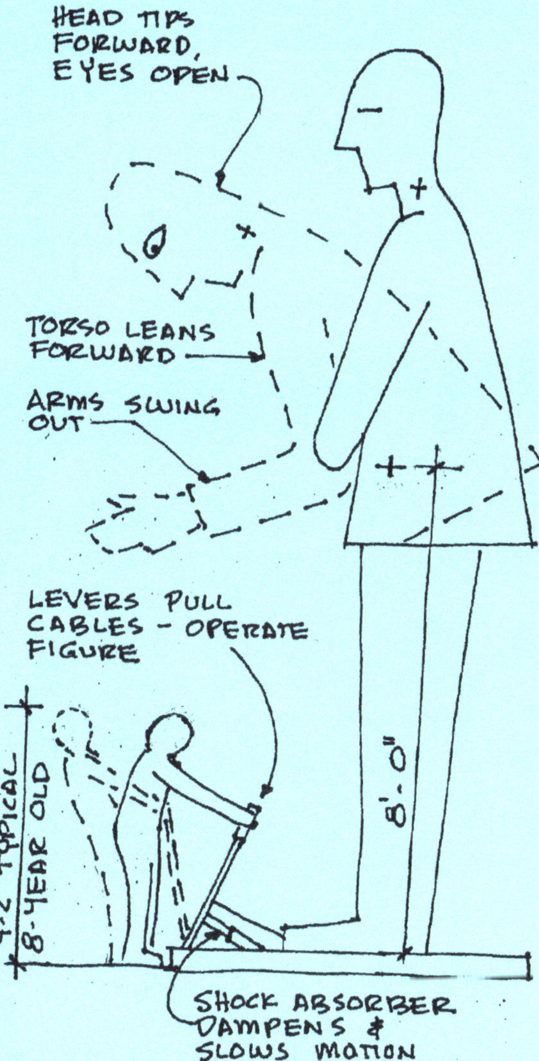

GIANT

½" = 1'-0"

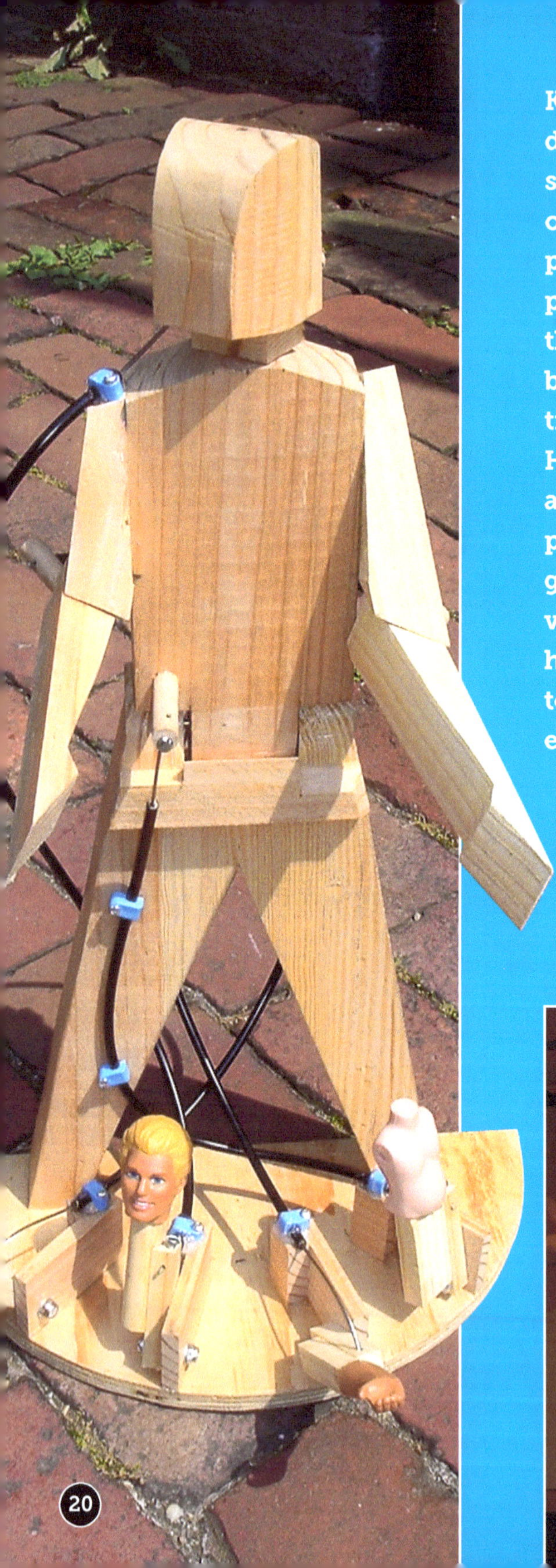

Kids were immediately
drawn to this wooden
sculpture, pulling hard
on the levers to make the
parts move. Through this
process, David observed
that his original plan would
be too complicated and
time consuming to execute.
His final piece was really
about letting small kids feel
powerful by controlling the
giant man. While he was
very interested in the details,
he edited his work down
to the essential parts of the
experience: the levers and a
simplified, abstracted body.

—Anne Fullenkamp

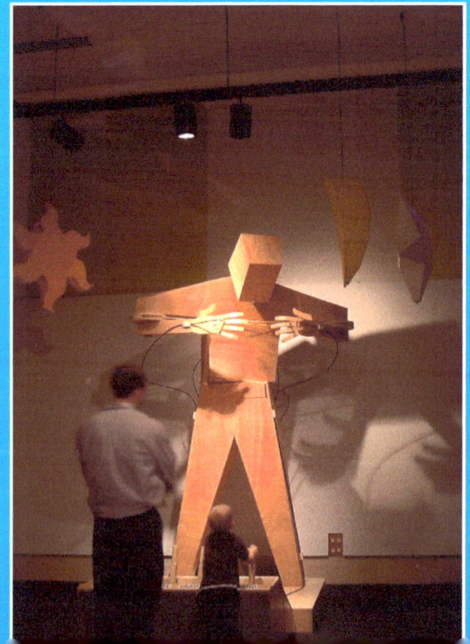

PROTOTYPICAL PROTOTYPING

Prototyping as Conversation

Kids making their way through the Children's Museum on a typical summer day might stumble across an official sign on a portable stanchion that reads,

WE ARE PROTOTYPING IDEAS FOR AN UPCOMING EXHIBIT. Let us know what you think.

While the term "prototype" may be familiar to some visitors as an object that isn't 100% complete, this instance might be the first time they see it refer to an activity. Prototyp*ing* is a special event at the Museum that brings the process of making art into the public space and turns it into an interactive experience all visitors are invited to both observe and participate. Even if kids don't immediately follow the sign's meaning, they are usually intrigued by the experiment going on

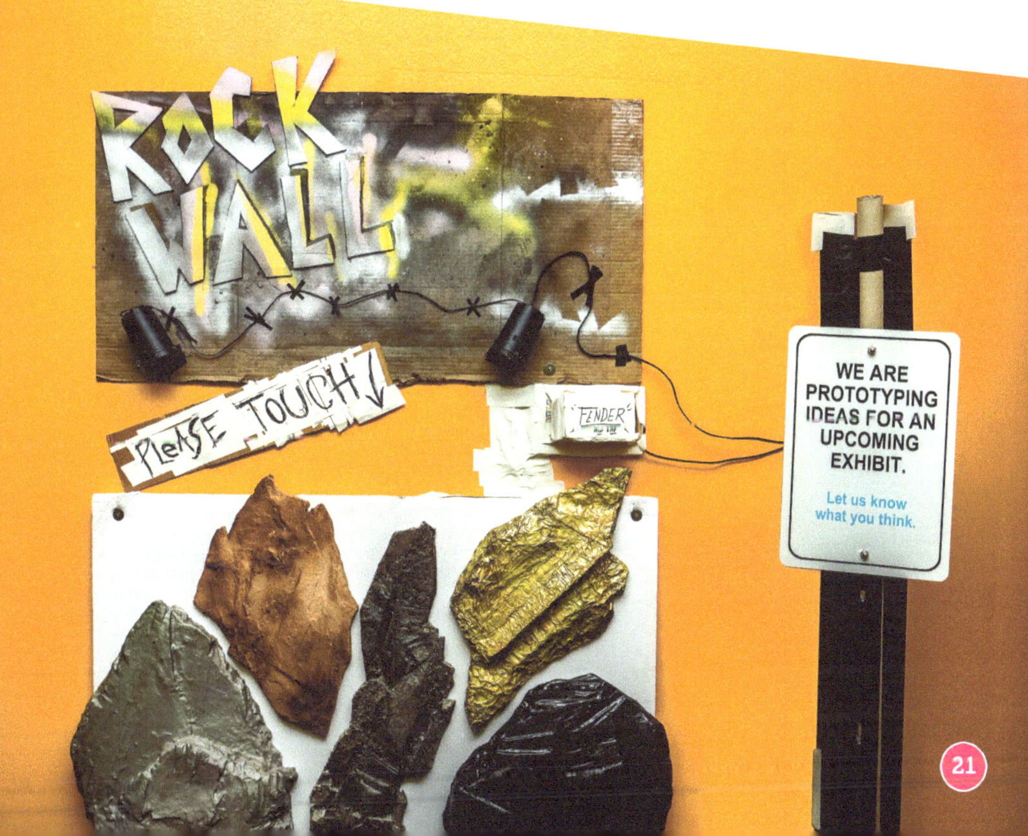

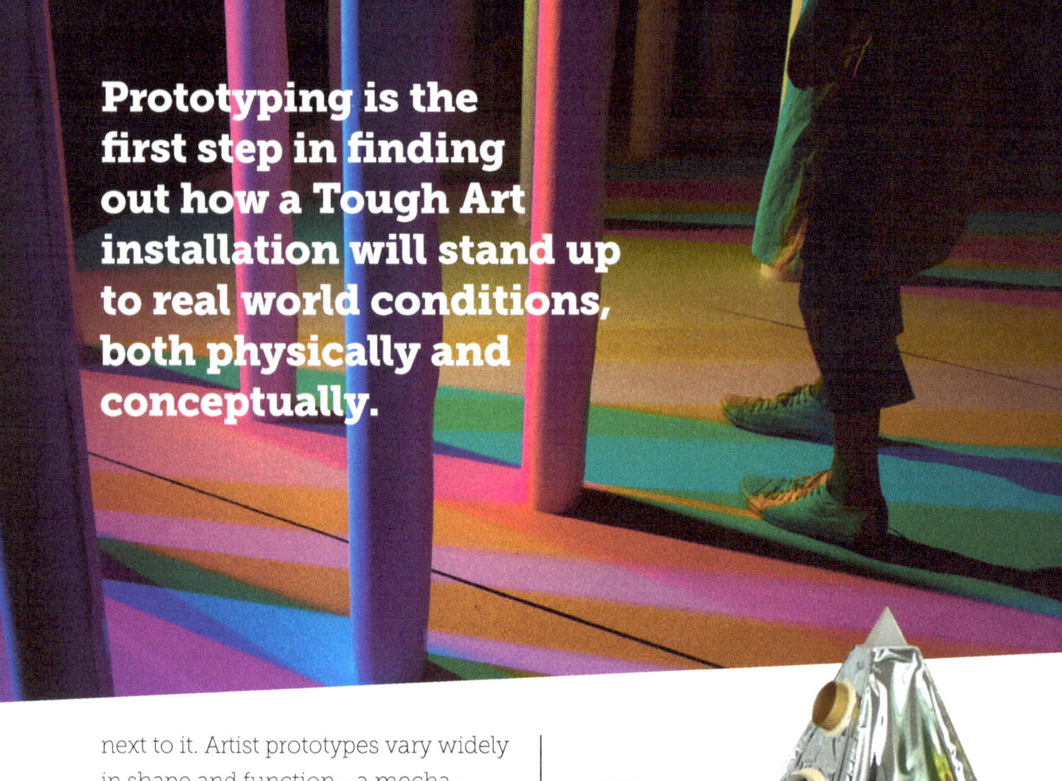

Prototyping is the first step in finding out how a Tough Art installation will stand up to real world conditions, both physically and conceptually.

next to it. Artist prototypes vary widely in shape and function—a mechanism, a software program, or even an idea; almost anything that needs to be put to a test. Kids have been asked to explore a two-and-a-half-foot tall, reflective pyramid; experiment with an interactive projection displaying a pile of colorful circles with eyes; and engage with metallic-looking rocks tacked to styrofoam underneath a hand-written plea to "Please touch."

Prototyping is the first step in finding out how a Tough Art installation will stand up to real world conditions, both physically and conceptually. In this case, the "real world" is an environment cultivated to encourage kids to play, experiment, and explore without worrying too much about rules and limitations. When actively prototyping in the Museum, artists and staff members carefully observe—sometimes from a distance and other times sitting cross-legged in the middle of the action—as kids press buttons, pick up pieces, fiddle with knobs, jump around, swing their arms wildly, and generally *interact* with whatever has been placed in front of them.

The prototyping process very much depends on the personality of the artist. Some artists like to talk to the children before, during, or after their interaction. *Is that too loud? What does that feel like? What did you want to do when you saw that shape?* Some artists feel more comfortable engaging with caretakers who have more experience reading their children's specific cues (after all, a parent might know better if a scrunched face and a shriek signals delight, disgust, or maybe both). Even if no talking occurs, the prototyping process is a conversation: the artist has articulated their creative hypothesis in a material form, and they listen to their young interlocutors' responses.

Depending on the artist's process and the type of artwork being produced, prototyping can lead to a wide array of conversations. Some revolve around the practical concerns that need to

new experience. However, most of the artists embrace this unique opportunity to have candid and honest feedback and listen carefully to their audiences' point of view.

The prototyping process is iterative. Once the artist hears and sees how kids are engaging with the prototype, they can respond in kind, and the conversation might take place over weeks. The next prototype might include a more complex mechanism or, alternatively, it might entail scaling back something that kids previously found confusing or difficult to hold. Perhaps the successive prototype

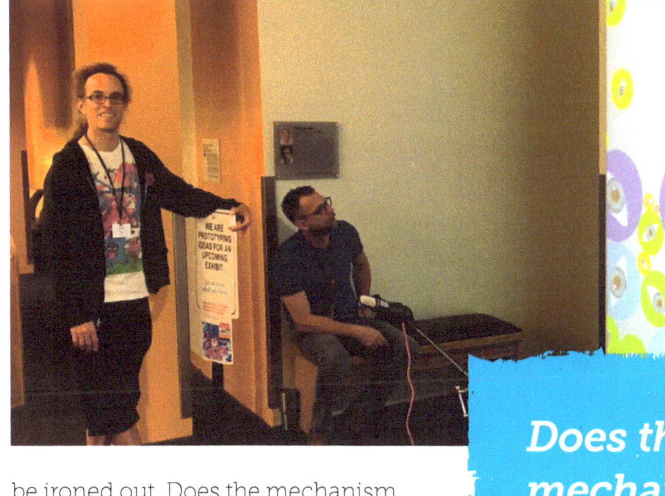

be ironed out. Does the mechanism work? Are the components too big or too small? Is this strong enough to hold up under pressure? Are the images comprehensible? There are also conversations about the artists' aesthetic choices, like the colors, materials, and even fundamental ideas. This can feel personal and even uncomfortable for the artist, especially if working with children in this way is a

Does the mechanism work? Are the components too big or too small? Is this strong enough to hold up under pressure?

will be a larger, more robust version of the previous version. In many instances, the next prototypes involve a completely unrelated component or a new idea altogether.

This conversation—the Children's Museum's process of prototyping—is probably the most critical ingredient for making a successful Tough Art piece. But prototyping can be hard, and progress can be slow. Watching a carefully crafted idea fall flat or literally break into pieces is humbling. Most of our artists have never undergone such a hands-on, open-ended critique. The only expectation artists should have going into a prototyping session is that kids will do something unexpected, something the artists would never have foreseen from the vantage point of their studios. There

is a clear correlation between consistent prototyping and those Tough Art installations that are ultimately well received and durable enough to hold their spot in the exhibit gallery. Likewise, the less successful Tough Art pieces—those that didn't stay intact for very long or perhaps lacked visitor engagement—almost always needed more prototyping. It is our job to help the artists see the distinctive artistic function of prototyping in this way.

Prototyping as Empathy

For some artists—including some of our Tough Artists—prototyping might at first seem like an intrusion into their artistic autonomy. After all, in one way

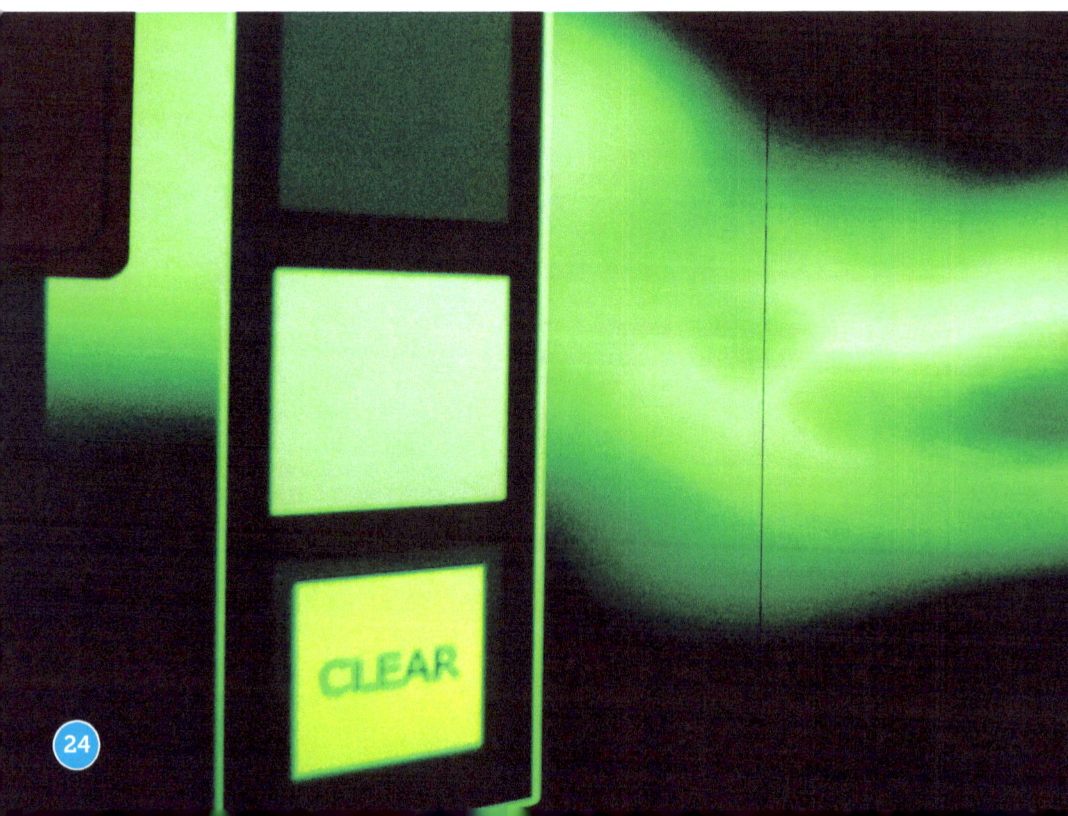

prototyping could be seen as a focus group for testing some mass-market product. Tough Artist Blaine Siegel (2010), for one, expressed his initial trepidation over the need to "compromise" between "being true to [his] art and [creating] an interactive art piece

We see prototyping in quite a different light. This process gives our young audience the respect they deserve by engaging them in the conversation as peers. Most museum art does not directly address children, and creating art aimed at kids requires special

We see prototyping in quite a different light. This process gives our young audience the respect they deserve by engaging them in the conversation as peers.

that works in the [Museum]."
Is the artist compromising their vision by testing their ideas? Are we compelling our artists to pander?

considerations. The art needs to come to this audience's level, both figuratively and literally. If a wall painting is simply too high for a child to see, lowering it to their sightline is about

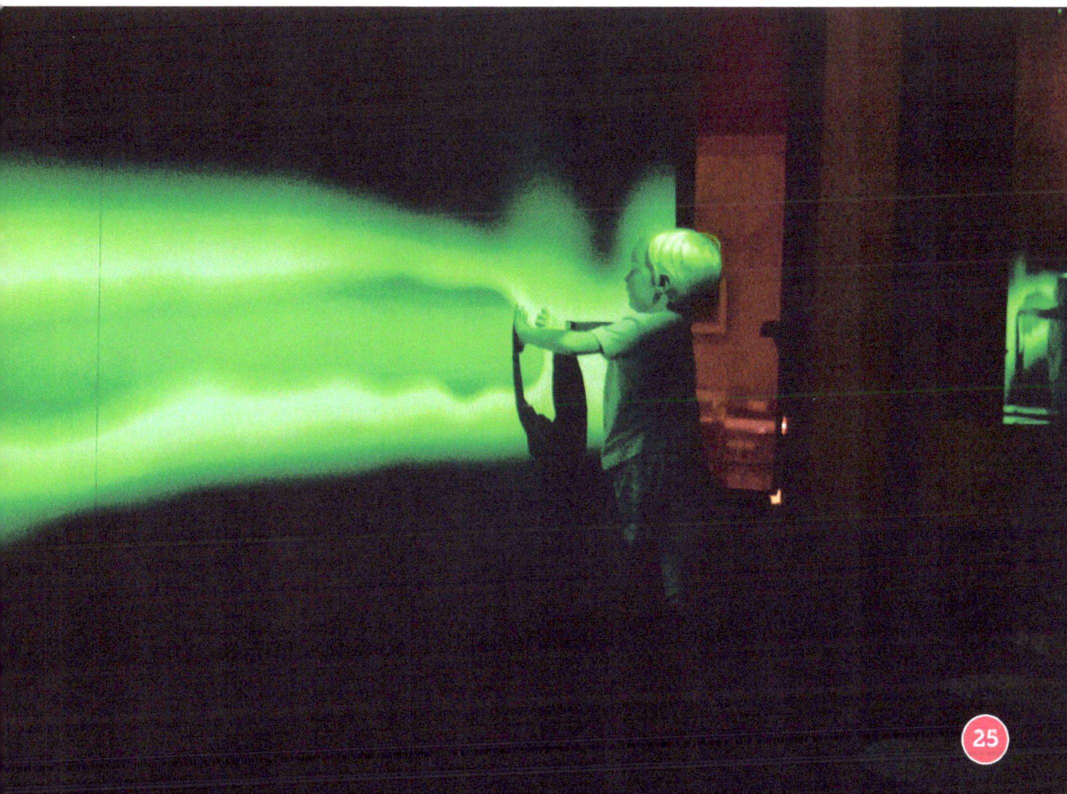

accessibility, which is quite different from pandering. We still want these artworks to challenge, provoke, excite, and inspire our young audiences like any successful interactive artwork. In order to do that, the artworks must be available to them.

Prototyping is a process that enables our artists to empathize with their young audiences, an act that can result in amazing creative implications. Beyond allowing artists to see from a child's perspective, the process enables artists to rediscover a childhood perspective that most adults lose as we become acculturated into rules and the hidden-in-plain-sight signs that tell us what to do—where to cross the street, which button to press in an elevator, what not to touch at an art museum. Where an adult sees a velvet rope hanging between stanchions as a sign to go no further, a child sees something soft and colorful to pull on and swing from. We can unlearn the learned behaviors that cloud our vision if we fully embrace the possibilities our young audiences embrace.

Meaningful art has always been about getting us to see the world in the manner a child sees it, where everything within is somewhat unfamiliar and full of possibility. Bringing artists and children together is about the confluence of two like-minded groups defined in part by how they both operate against the stale conventions that most of us have come

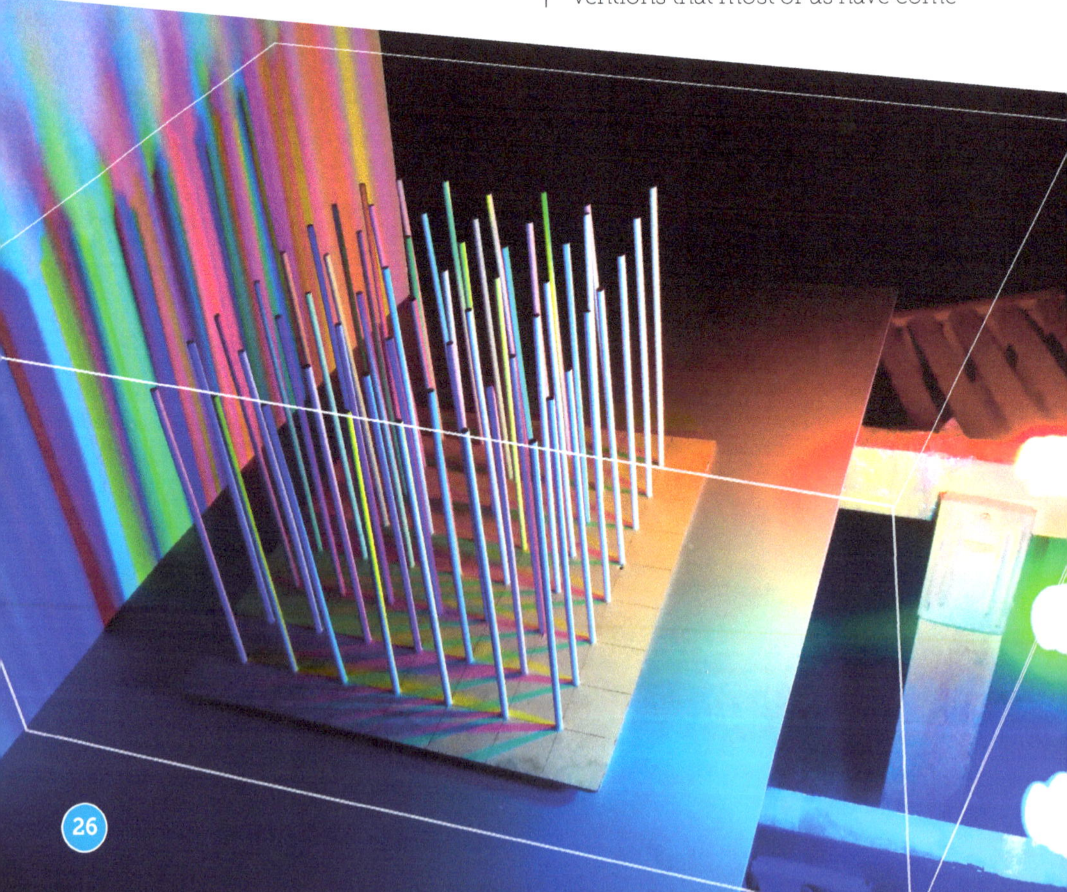

to see as natural, normal, and inevitable. The child may not yet see the rules and limitations, and the artist chooses to question them. They both have a lot to learn from each other.

Prototyping as Model

Prototyping is a core principle of Tough Art because it speaks to how the residency itself has responded and adapted over the years. Every iteration of Tough Art— new cohorts and new artists—is a prototype that we at the

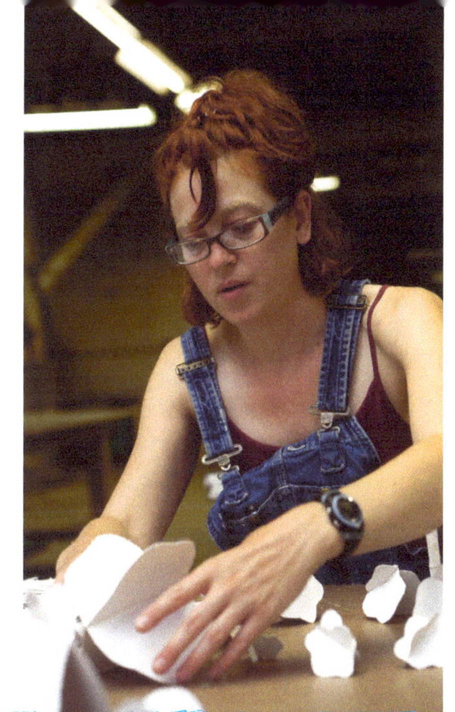

Museum can learn from. When an artwork catches our visitors' imagination, we want to know why. Every time an artist connects with their audience, we strive to understand that connection. Every time something breaks down, we want to figure out what happened and improve for the next time.

Just as we ask our artists to remain responsive to their audience's needs and abilities, it is equally important for the Tough Art program to remain responsive and avoid making the process too routine. After years of

trial and error, flexibility and adaptability are now built into the DNA of Tough Art and, really, everything that we do as a children's museum. This is a lesson we learn over and over again from our young audiences.

21: Early Prototype for *Cosmic Geometry* (Owen Lowery, 2019)

22: (Top) Prototype for *Prism Palace* (Lindsey Packer, 2014)

22: (Btm) Prototype for *Pyramids* (Chris Beauregard, 2013)

23: Early prototype for *Mechanical Masterpieces* (Neil Mendoza, 2018)

24-25: Digital prototype for *Cosmic Geometry* (Owen Lowery, 2019)

26: Scale model prototype for *Prism Palace* (Lindsey Packer, 2014)

27: Scale model prototype for *the eXpedition* (Jennifer Van Winkle, 2009)

Jonathan Armistead
& Scott Andrew

KITTY KIDDIE MEOW MEOW

Spreading Joy

When I look back on some of the Tough Art projects, I wonder: was that art, an experience, or something else? For some projects I could never quite decide. *Kitty Kiddie Meow Meow* was one of those. The two artists, Scott Andrew and Jonathan Armistead, were wonderful people—enthusiastic and fun. When I first met them at Carnegie Mellon University, they were doing a project with glitter.

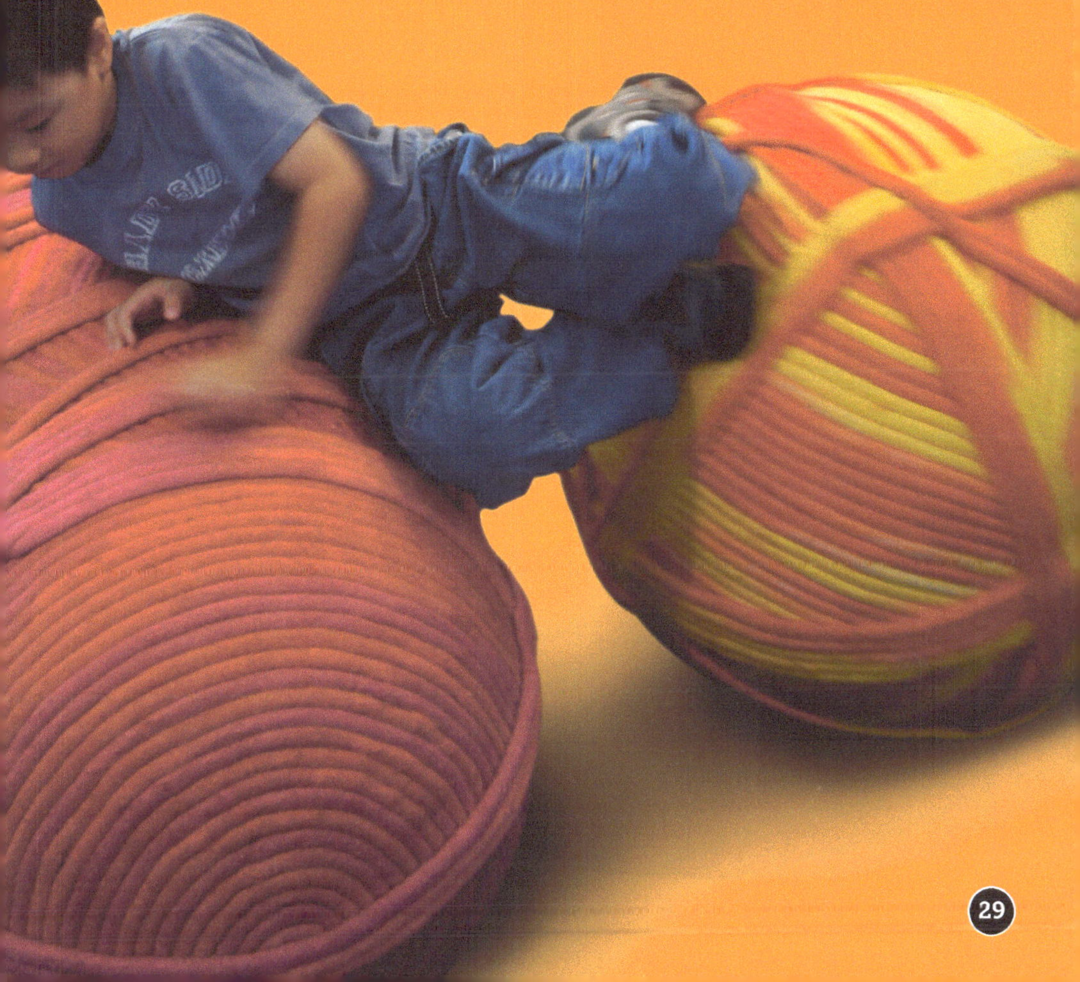

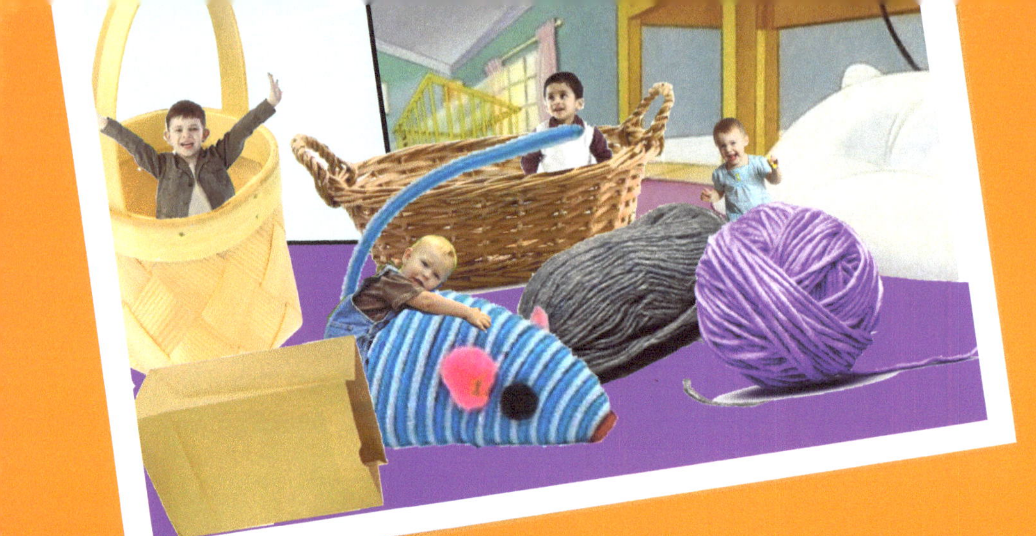

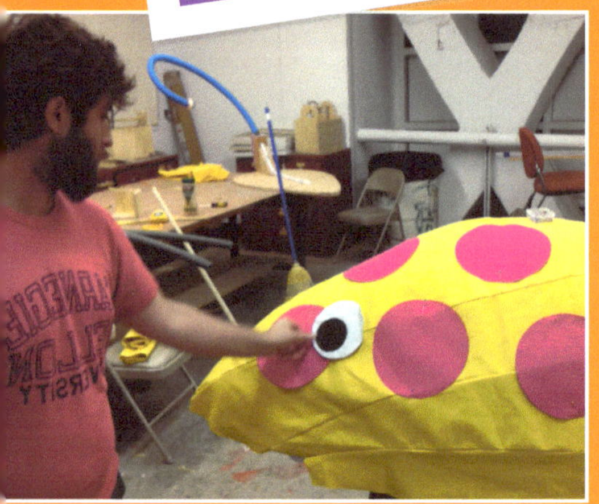

I was

fascinated by the glitter and thought, this is just awesome and amazing.

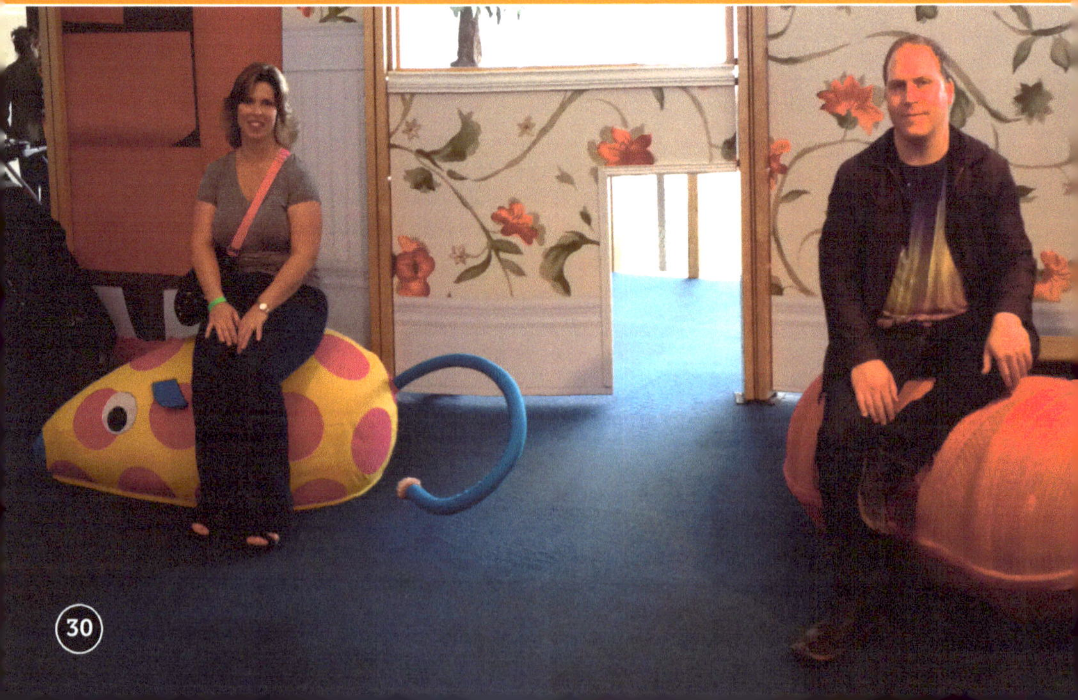

It wasn't just a little bag of glitter; it was a giant barrel of glitter. I was fascinated by the glitter and thought, this is just awesome and amazing.

For Tough Art, they created an environment in which the visitors were the cats, so everything was enlarged—a giant ball of yarn, a giant basket, and a giant mouse toy. They also partnered with the Humane Society who came in for an event with real cats available for adoption at the Museum once the exhibit was open. It was kind of wonderful.

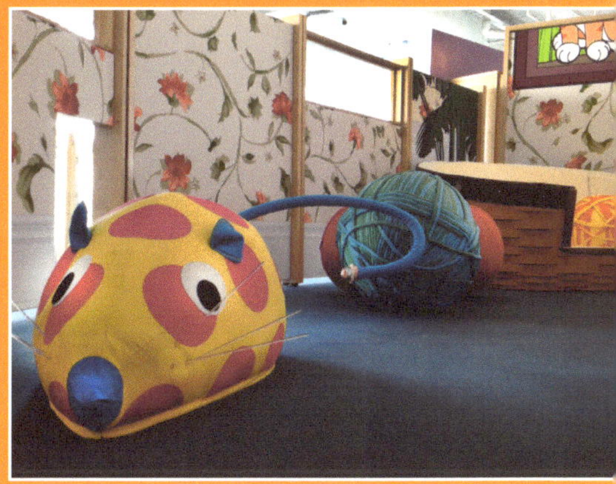

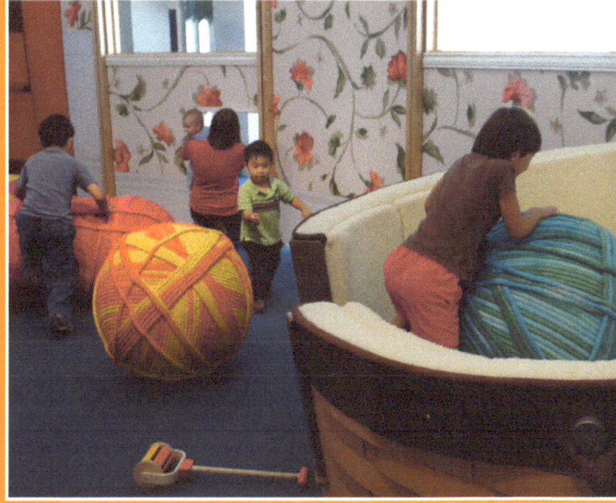

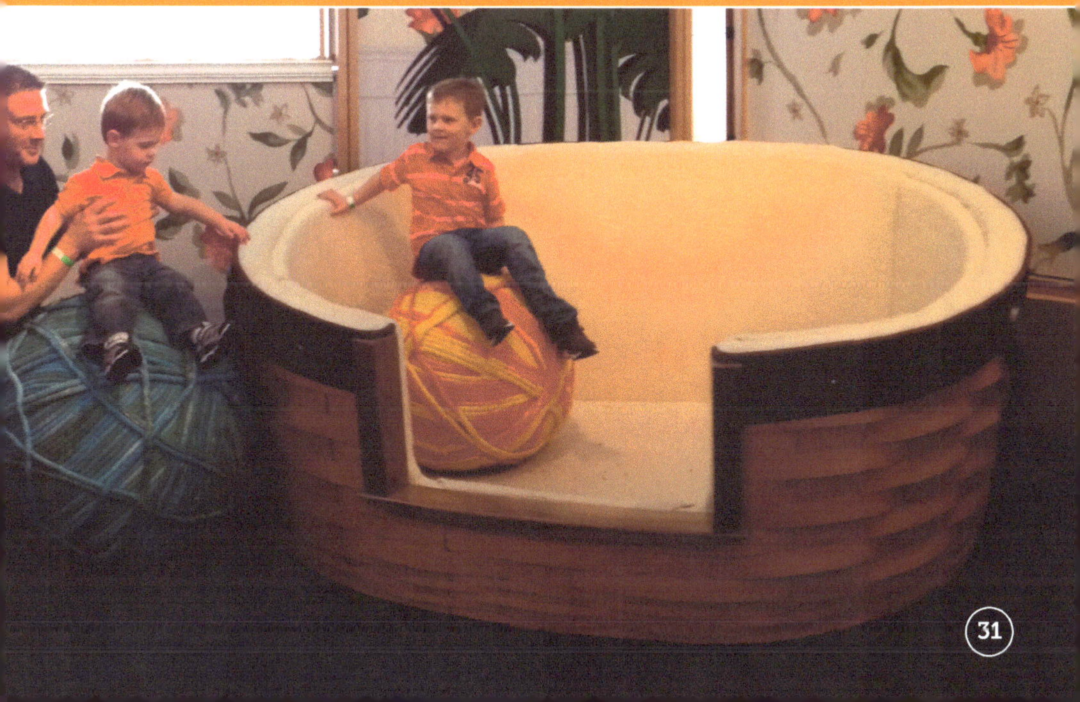

During their residency, the artists were also collecting cat T-shirts, which they'd wear every time they came to work at the Museum. They had so many that we did an additional exhibit in which we hung twenty of their cat T-shirts on a wall in a semi formal display. The whole thing—the giant cat toy environment, the cats for adoption, the cat T-shirt display—was all beyond the usual categories for a Tough Art work, but it was really great.

—*Penny Lodge*

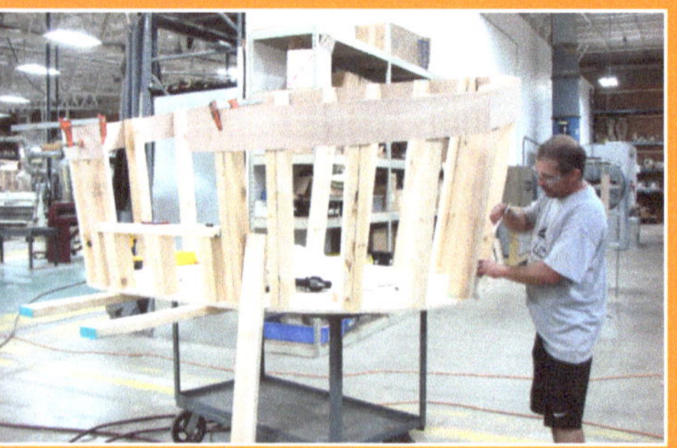

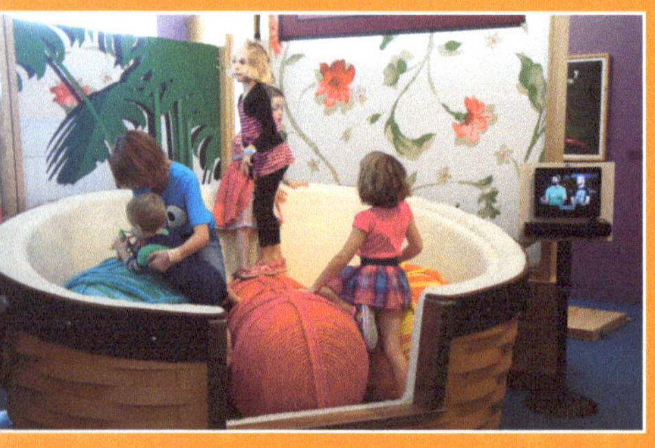

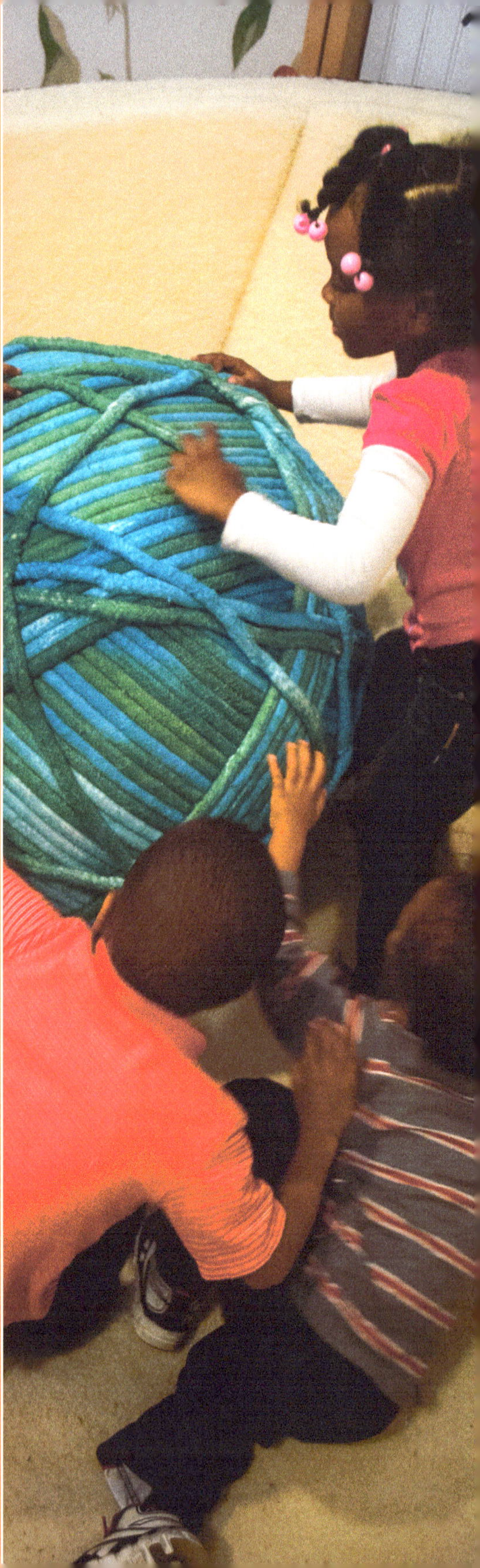

ARTISTS' REFLECTIONS

Considering Younger Audiences

Shohei Katayama
Nimbus Drum (2017)

Learning a range of behaviors from toddlers to adults changed *Nimbus Drum*'s physical shape: introducing borders to reduce cleaning, adding a theatrical environment, having multiple magnets to prevent conflict between "users." I think the tactile nature of the work's interaction made it successful. Kids love noise, touching things, and experiences that are engaging.

Zach Dorn
The Honorable and Bewhiskered Herman Hibel (2011)

Not only did these young visitors wield the power of candid criticism, they were also bursting with creative spirit. My imagination went into hyperdrive and inspired me to attempt to create a space that suspended reality.

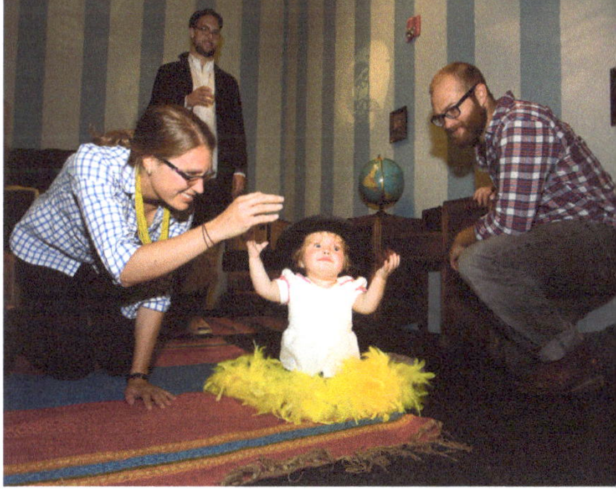

Ibiyinka Alao
Painting Light (2020)
(Tough Art @Home)

When we are children, we don't understand things like shading and shadow in drawing or painting. To teach, I have to remember my own process of learning when I was a child and the discoveries we make as children. One of these is how light plays tricks on our eyes. The discovery of how light actually works is pure joy.

Blaine Siegel
Aerophone (2010)

Spending time at the Museum reminded me of how children engage with things. If you give them one thing with an intended use, they will find five other uses. I was reminded of the way they look at the world and their open-mindedness. I saw how literally tough children can be on things, to the point of being destructive. But at the same time, they are very creative.

The Impact of Prototyping

Owen Lowery

I loved prototyping. It was the most beneficial aspect of the residency. It made a huge difference. Honestly, when people bend and break your stuff, it's gut-wrenching when you're in the middle of it. But when something cracks or splits or whatever, you understand that you were too light on testing it and need to make things stronger.

Megan Flød Johnson
The NEST (2017)

I prototyped with a lot of playing and different kinds of communication.

I recall there was a young boy, who came to visit *The NEST*. The boy wasn't super verbal, and he was really fascinated with the boots I was wearing. We started imagining what kind of shoes *The NEST*'s creature would wear. It turned into this dance of communication around *The NEST*. He would try something and then I would mimic it and then he would laugh. We developed this whole choreography.

Eunice Choi
Tomato Medley (2019)

The prototyping process was the biggest challenge during the residency. I was overthinking my decisions and felt a huge pressure to try out prototypes in the museum space. I worried too much about what would be a "good" prototype to test and having "finished" prototypes, which is the opposite of what a prototype should be.

The Tough Art experience helped me reflect on my relationship with

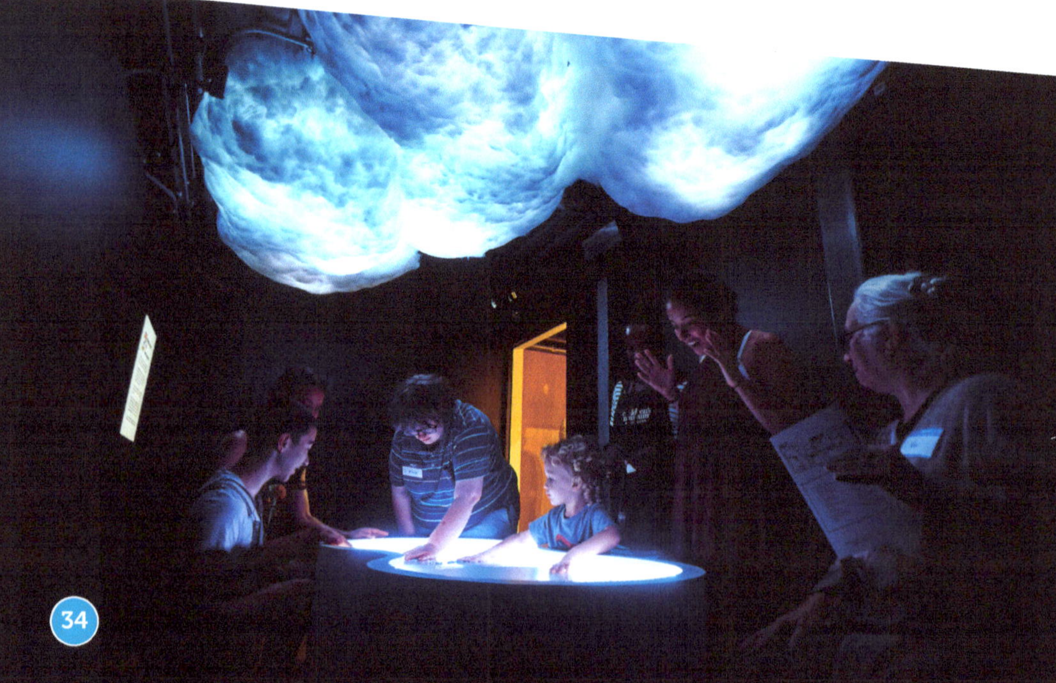

process, audience, and practice. I learned that it is important to accept the process as its own project, instead of worrying about evaluating each stage of the process.

very weighty evolved into something more linear and lighter. That was a big change from my typical process. In the Museum, you start with one idea, and you have to stay receptive to the

Zach Dorn

My original concept for the Tough Art residency embraced this tech-savvy character for myself, proposing a digital projection project that would transport footage of visitors into miniature dioramas. Within a few days of prototyping, that concept faded fast. The kids couldn't overlook my amateur technological skills. Their ability to confront exhibitions with vigor and earnest curiosity demanded that my work actually function. It didn't take a peer critique to tell me I wasn't a new media artist, just five minutes with a six-year-old.

Blaine Siegel

With my first prototype, the kids took the hose and started blowing it all around. I thought about how wonderful and how beautiful it was. Seeing this also started to influence the form of *Aerophone*. A form that was initially more amorphous and

work. There are a lot of things you need to pay attention to—the space, the work, the nature of making this thing that children can interact with yet will still conceive of as an artwork.

The Museum's Guidance

Jenna Boyles

I felt supported by the Museum staff, and they had faith in me. I mentioned that I had welded once before and their response was, *Okay, go forth and weld*, and so I was able to use the Museum's welding equipment.

I built the majority of it on my own, but I also understood that this was a large scale piece that I couldn't do entirely by myself. I asked for help when I needed it, and I did need others to help when it was time to install the big structure. The experience gave

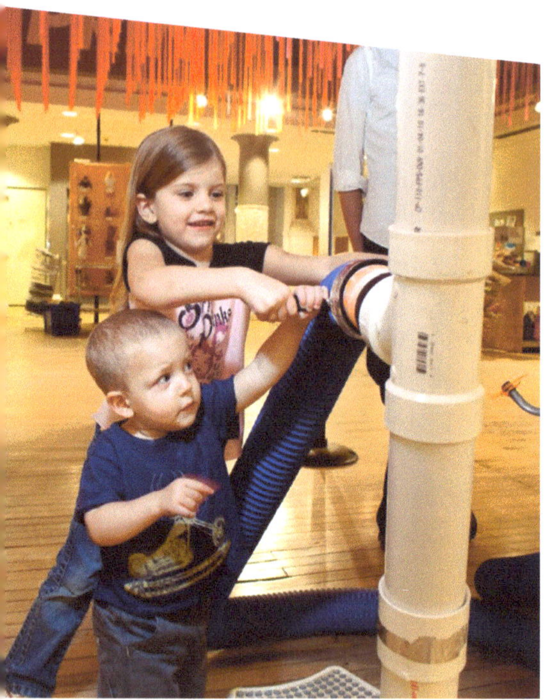

me the confidence to judge when I could take a self-directed approach and learn along the way and when I needed to ask for assistance.

That was something I definitely learned from the residency— how much do I personally take on versus when it makes sense to ask for help or delegate.

Owen Lowery

I'm not used to support in the way I had at the Museum. I'm good at being playful and childlike with people, and I'm used to people not really being able to picture the ideas I have in my head. But being around a group of people who enjoyed the working process, really listened and thought about ideas, and gave input that was aimed at truly making a better piece was strangely difficult for me to understand and take in at first.

Shohei Katayama

People from different departments with different expertise participated in critiques. This allowed me to hear multiple perspectives, which helped me frame how the work can exist in the broader museum world.

Ibiyinka Alao

Tough Art @home was one of the first times that I have used video conferencing. Lacey [Murray, Tough Art program manager] set up the video call and recorded it. She became my audience, listening and reacting as I showed the activity. The Museum wanted to try this experiment and they encouraged me to try too.

Blaine Siegel

The Tough Art Orientation week gave me a new perspective on the residency and the differences between designing exhibits for others versus creating art for oneself. From then on, it was an ongoing dialogue in my mind. I started off feeling that I needed to compromise what I wanted to do, and that I needed to make it a "tough" design. That wasn't what I typically did, but it was necessary to make *Aerophone* work at the Museum.

Megan Flød Johnson

I think you need a caring attitude from the staff for this kind of program. You need people that can connect with the artists. When I first met the staff for the residency, they served as mentors and after the residency we have stayed in touch. It has been a really invaluable relationship for me.

Insights from Being a Tough Artist

Jenna Boyles

My Tough Art experience really opened up my sense of potential in regard to the scale and durability of sculptural projects. I also learned that when I am presented with a challenge—in this case an artwork for children—I enjoy figuring out how to bring my own personal vision to the work.

Owen Lowery

I figured out that the meaning in my work is creating opportunities for people to take actions that support habits of mind—such as curiosity, discovery—considering that there's more to something than what's on the surface. I didn't realize that I was trying to create habits in people before this summer, but constantly creating and testing got me there.

Blaine Siegel

There's nothing wrong with creating specifically for children. I can do this in an approach consistent with my work. It helped me recognize how to balance what I create for myself and what I create for someone else.

Ibiyinka Alao

The online video has helped me. People search my name, find it, and watch it. For example, I taught an in-person lesson for a group of kids and learned that they had already done my Tough Art @Home exercise with their moms. These reactions are very humbling. You record the lesson once and then you know they can play it over and over again. At the beginning, I didn't think I would be able to create a video lesson. Now I know it's possible.

Megan Flød Johnson

Usually residencies are, *We have this much money, in this time window, and we're looking for this outcome.* This has given me more confidence to go into relationships with other institutions and not be afraid to ask for what I need. Even if the answer is *No*, I am now more willing to ask.

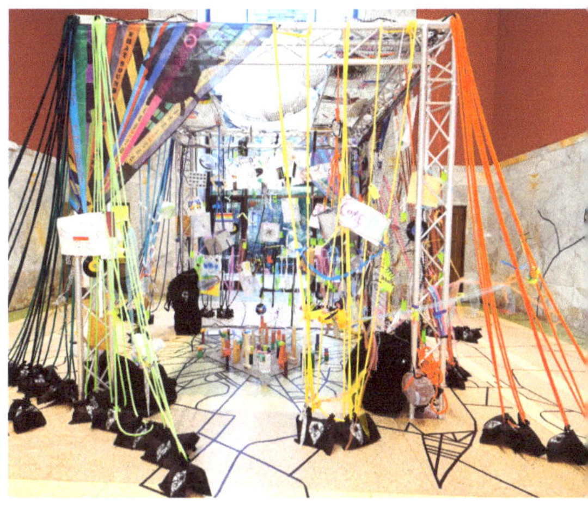

Shohei Katayama

From the residency I learned how to have fun and that art doesn't need to cater only to people who visit a "white cube" gallery.

33: *The Honorable and Bewhiskered Herman Hibel* (Zach Dorn, 2011)
34: *Nimbus Drum* (Shohei Katayama, 2017)
36: *Aerophone* (Blaine Siegel, 2010)
37: *The NEST* (Megan Flød Johnson, 2017)

Scott Garner

REACH

Technical Magic

REACH is a large, low relief mural consisting of star-and moon-shaped electronic pads that produce musical tones when touched simultaneously.

Scott was inspired by Pittsburgh as a city of bridges; his idea of spanning or reaching across a space came directly from the city's skyline.

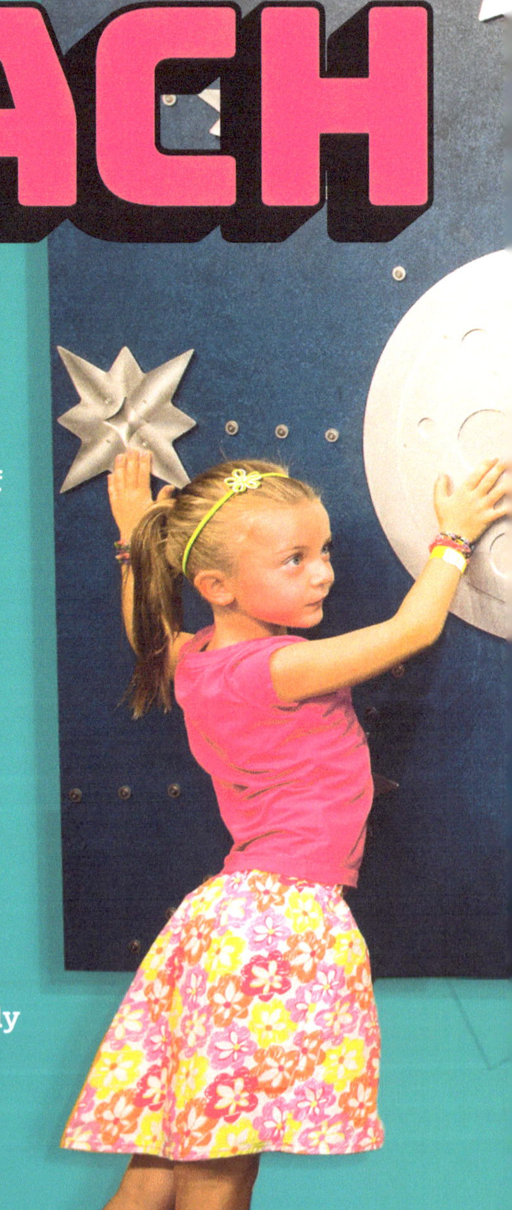

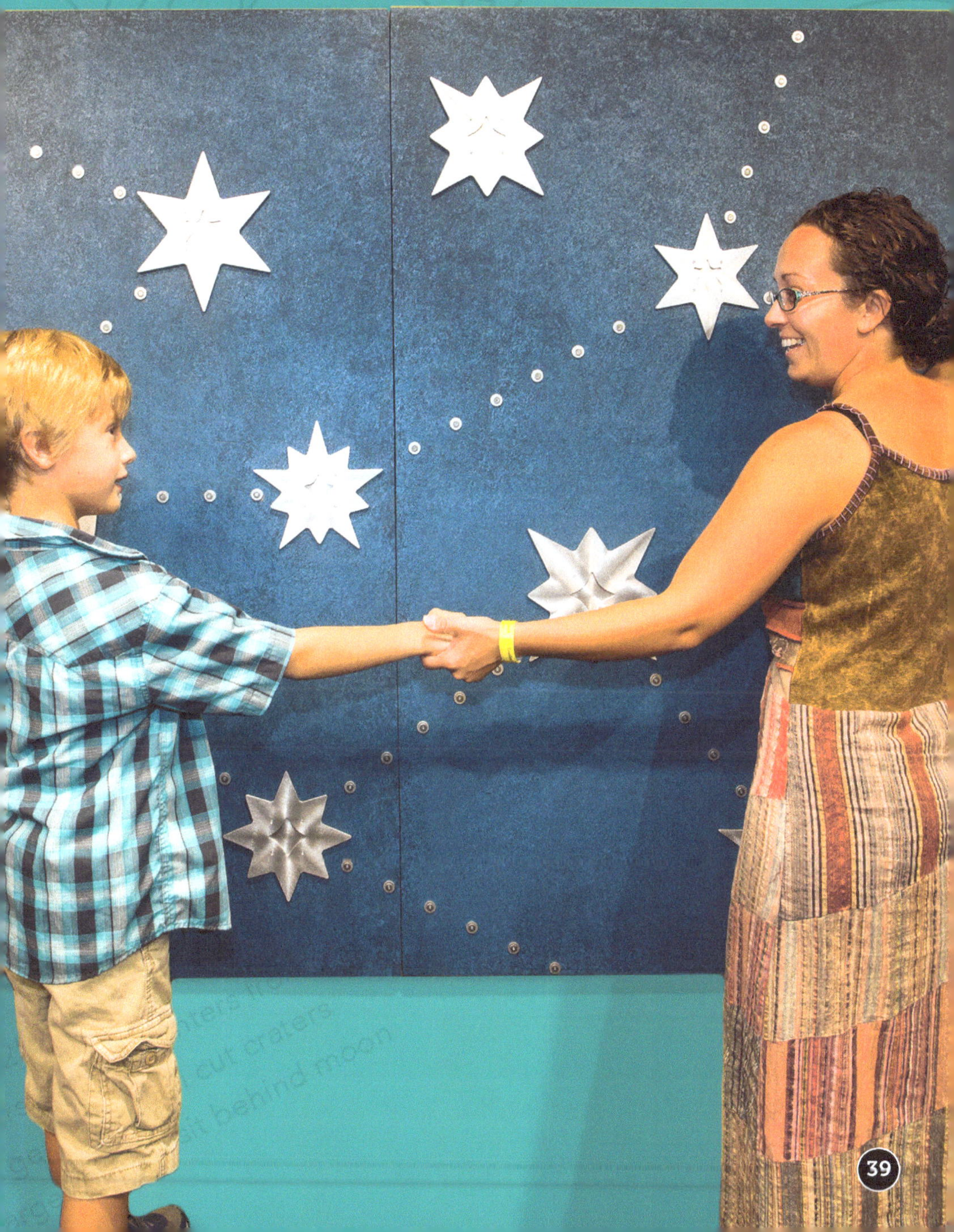

raters fr
ut craters
it behind moon

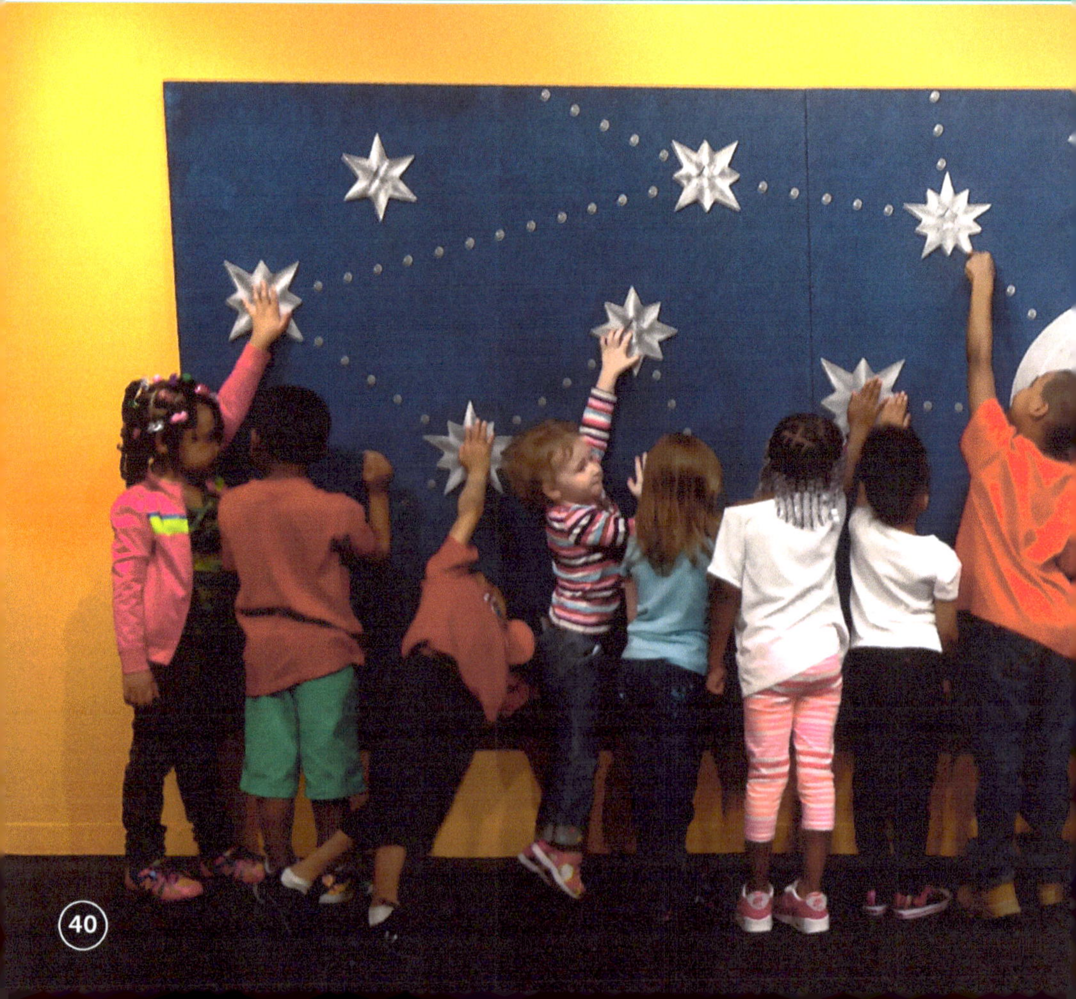

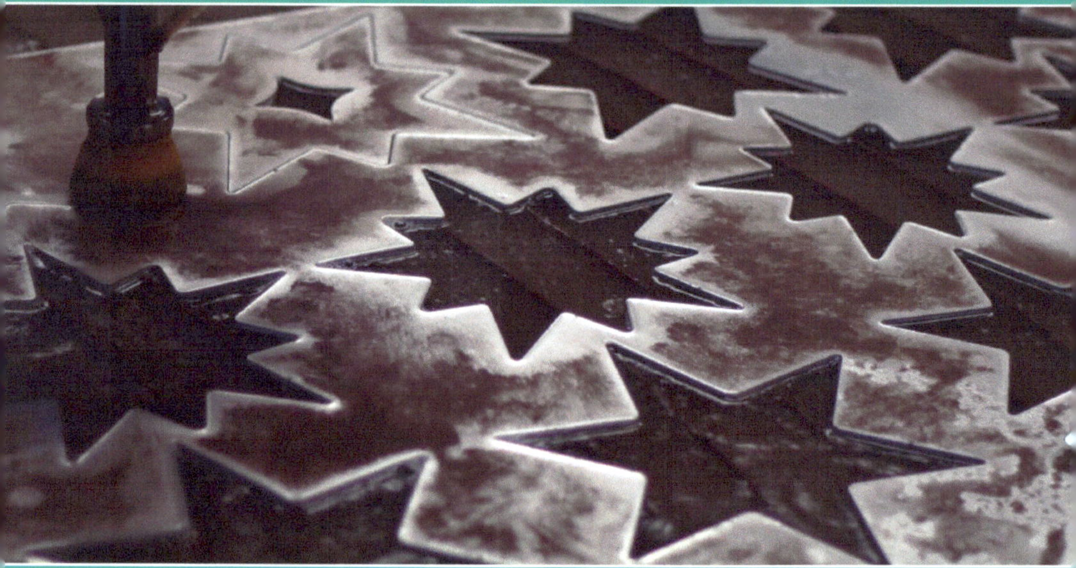

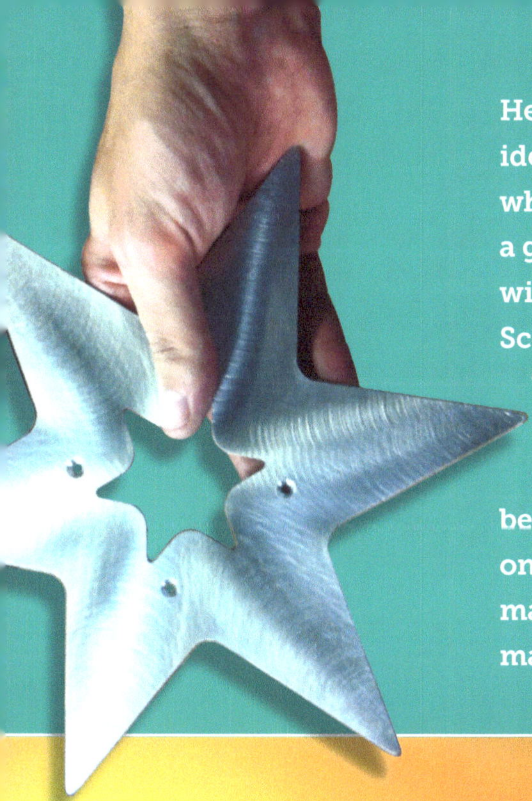

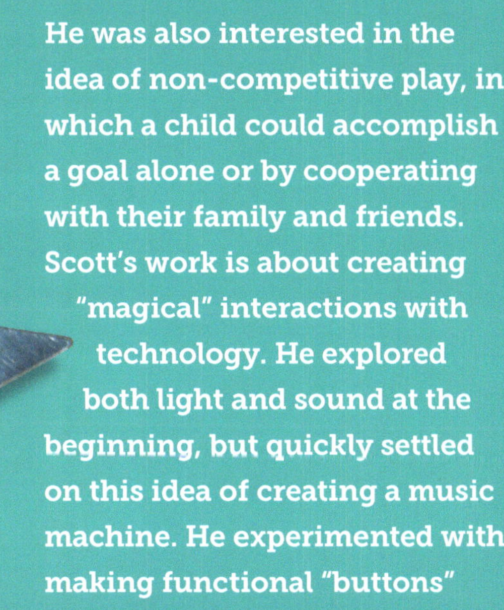

He was also interested in the idea of non-competitive play, in which a child could accomplish a goal alone or by cooperating with their family and friends. Scott's work is about creating "magical" interactions with technology. He explored both light and sound at the beginning, but quickly settled on this idea of creating a music machine. He experimented with making functional "buttons"

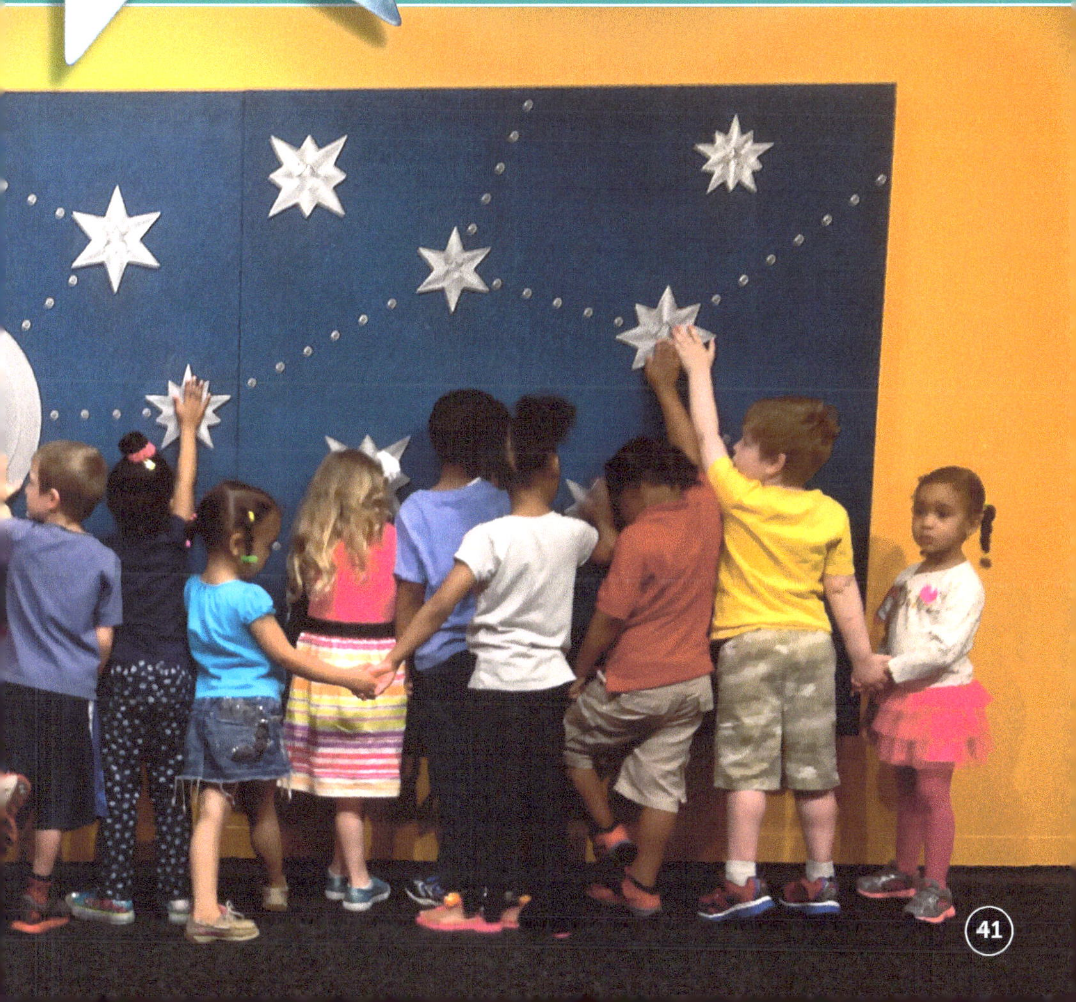

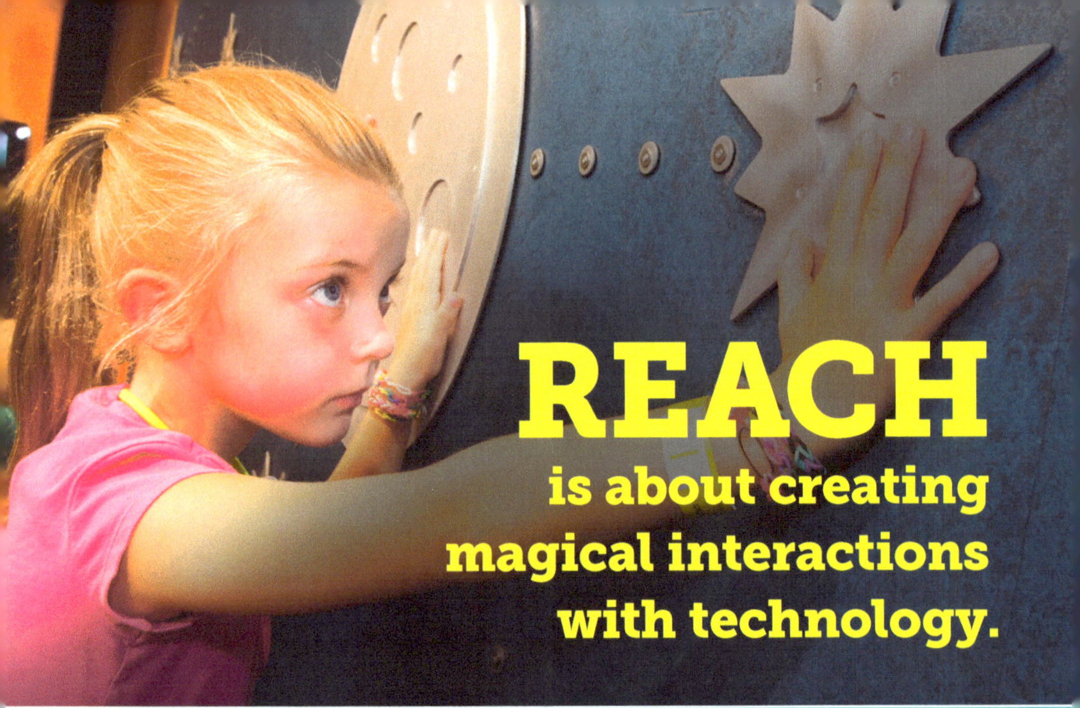

REACH

is about creating magical interactions with technology.

that didn't look like buttons, creating a sense of surprise when they triggered the music.

When someone touches one panel, nothing happens, but when they touch two at the same time, a musical note plays. If two or more people form a human chain by holding hands, and then each touches a panel, music plays, too. This was magical, surprising, and delightful.

The prototyping was about how to present it, where to put the sensors to make people know what to do and how to do it. The prototype used geometric shapes and colors for the touch pads. Touching a square and a circle doesn't sound as interesting as touching the moon and a star.

—*Anne Fullenkamp*

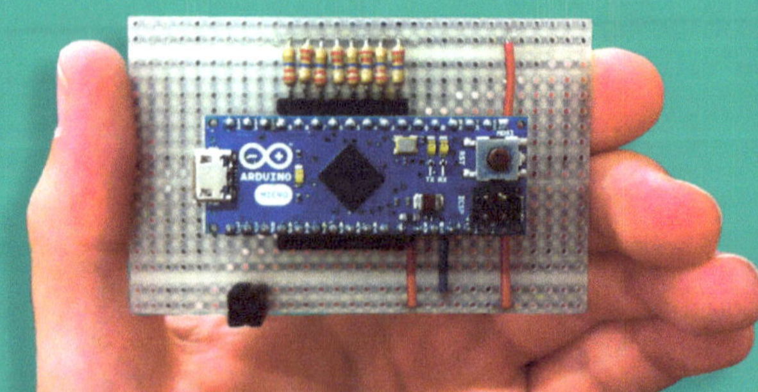

STAFF PERSPECTIVES

Tough Art's importance to the Museum

Greg Witt
(Senior Exhibit Designer and inaugural Tough Artist)

Many exciting new ideas in the Museum come from Tough Art. It's always a great break from the regular routine and a totally different energy.

Tough Art is also an ongoing investment in new work and artists. Exhibit development is expensive and Tough Art is neither more nor less expensive when viewed in that context. But it is also important that it gives funding and opportunity to a cohort of artists every year.

Lacey Murray
(Tough Art Manager since 2017)

With this happening every summer, we know to expect three to four fresh new pieces to put out for the visitors every year. If they're robust enough, some pieces stay after their Tough Art debut. Being able to expect new pieces every year is a nice benefit of the program.

Penny Lodge
(Former Exhibits Director)

The artists are really creative and come up with new ways to look at things. That's one of our philosophies in the Museum, looking at the world in a different way. And artists really help us to do that.

The mystery of it is that you never know what the result will be. You could find this amazing, joyful experience that you never expected. You don't discover those joyful things every time, but it is wonderful when you do.

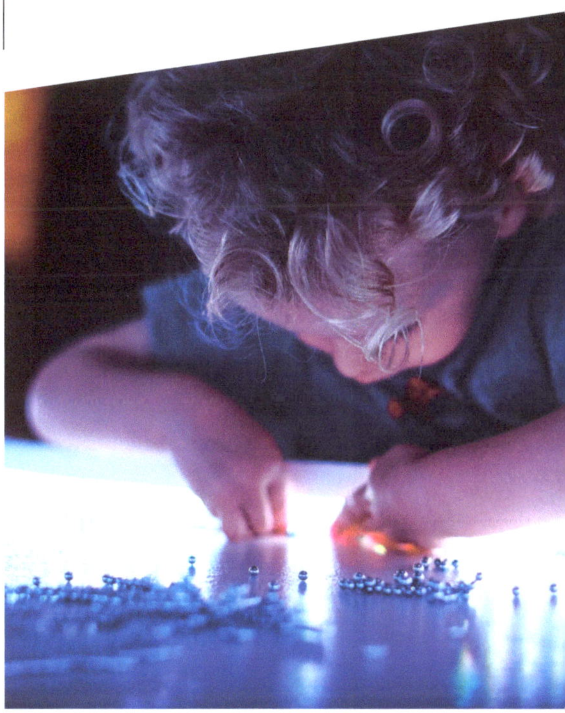

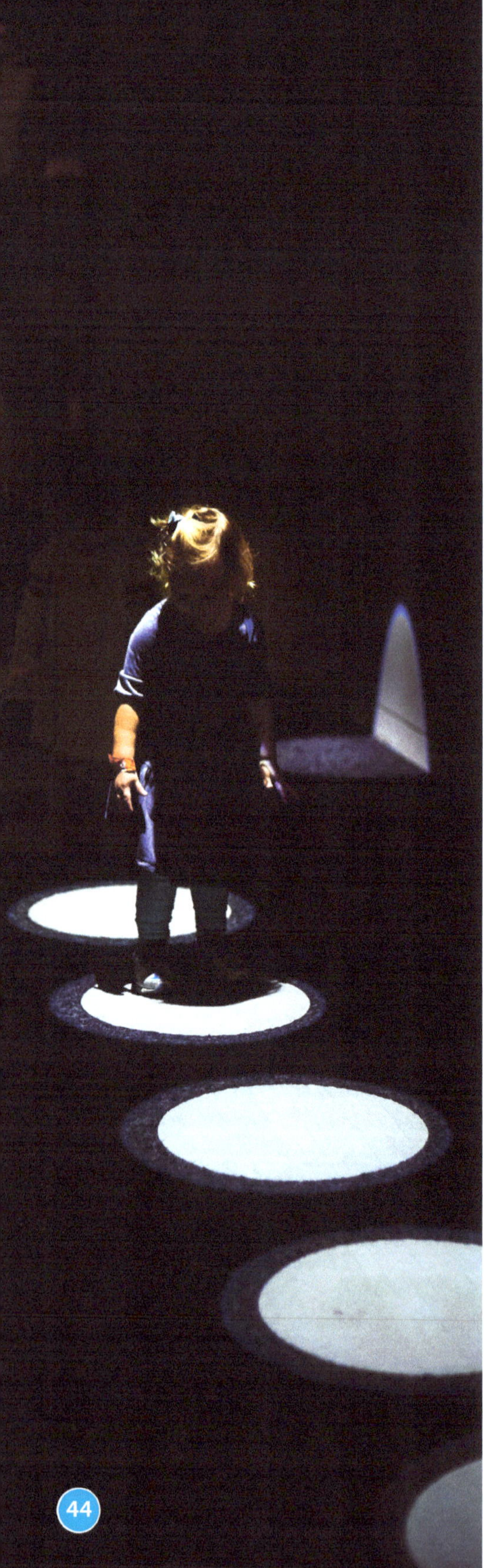

Jane Werner

(Executive Director)

We certainly are not the experts on many, many things. We know how to do "children's museum" things. There are so many other experts out there who know how to do great things for children and families outside the museum setting. Being open and inviting those experts to the children's museum and seeing what they do and how it relates to kids is always exciting. It's so important because you get stale fast. If your mission is to do the best for kids, then you want everyone to participate and bring their expertise and whole self to the endeavor.

How the program guides artists

Keny Marshall

(Former Exhibit Designer)

Tough Art is an opportunity for artists to meet and work alongside other artists. The synergy comes from this connection between the creativity of the artist cohort and the experience of the staff they work with.

Penny Lodge

At the beginning of the residency, we talk with the artists about what they are thinking. We take them on the Museum floor to observe the visitors, maybe speak with the visitors, and to understand what happens here daily, what four- and five-year-old kids do in the Museum and what their parents do. We try to make it very clear what resources are available at the Museum.

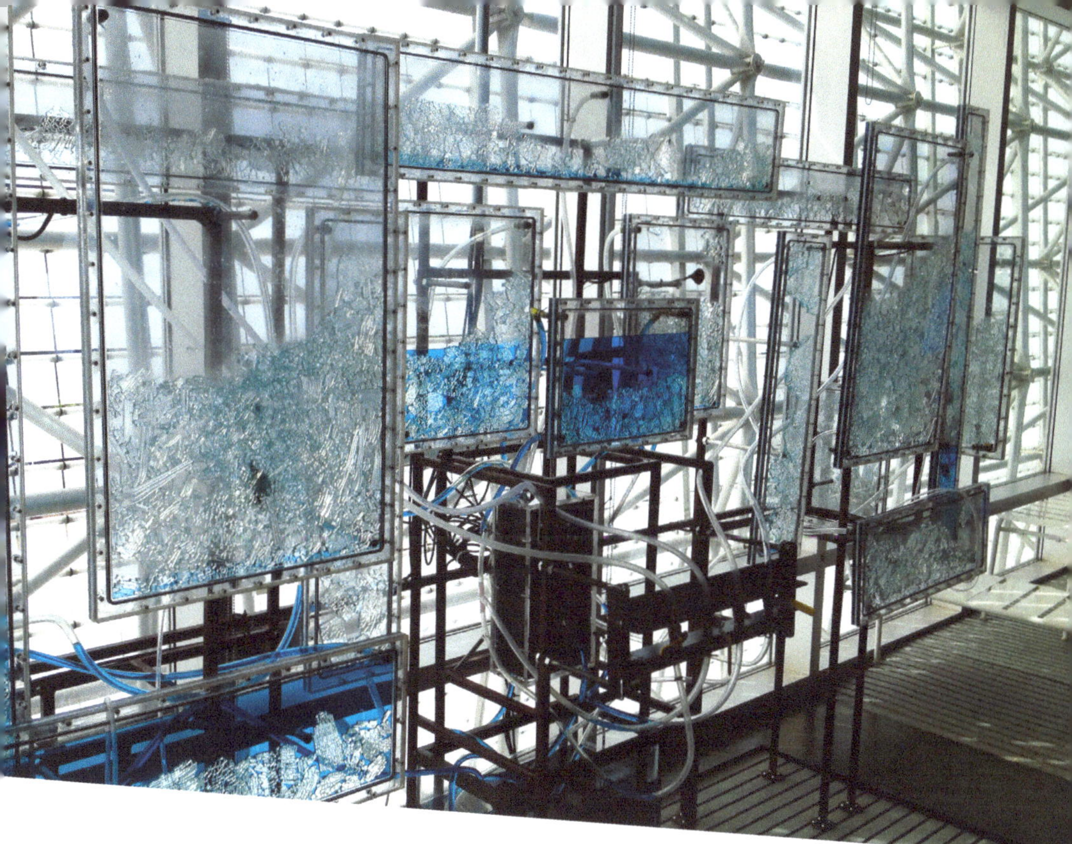

After that, it becomes more about, *How are you developing your idea?* And then, *How are you going to prototype your idea on the floor?* The next step is a plan to put a prototype on the floor on a specific day. As the summer progresses, we want less time discussing and more time prototyping and iterating your idea. Artists will work with our fabricators to make it tough enough, learn from them, and gain some experience.

Lacey Murray

During prototype testing, I have seen some really beautiful experiences and exchanges happen between visitors and artists. However, artists can also put their piece out and just observe from a distance. Because that's how their piece is going to be when it's installed—the artist isn't going to be there to host it.

Greg Witt

We try to balance the Museum's expectations with the artist's ambition and capability. We try to gauge what an artist is capable of in a given amount of time rather than having them pursue whatever wild thing. If time is running out, sometimes we try to steer them toward what we think is achievable, will last, or visitors are going to be into. At the same time, we try to steer artists away from building a "children's museum exhibit" and encourage them to create a work that fits into their practice.

On what makes for a good Tough Art installation

Keny Marshall

The challenge for the artists is to create unique, audience-tested work... understanding that there are different expectations in children's museums. Being experimental and taking risks is key along with the understanding that the end goal is to ensure the interactive experience is both meaningful and "tough". Making a robust and meaningful project requires working directly with children.

Children are rarely timid, and they interact in unexpected and un-careful ways.

Greg Witt

We can't really talk about what makes a good art project for the artists, but we can talk about what makes a good interaction and a good experience on the Museum floor. We talk with the artists about interaction design and how we judge whether an interactive is interesting or not.

We definitely get a lot of artists with limited experience. Sometimes it works out great, sometimes not so good. It's not the end of the world if some things don't work out, it's part of the game. Ultimately, we do end up with a lot of really cool work and quite a few are in our permanent collection.

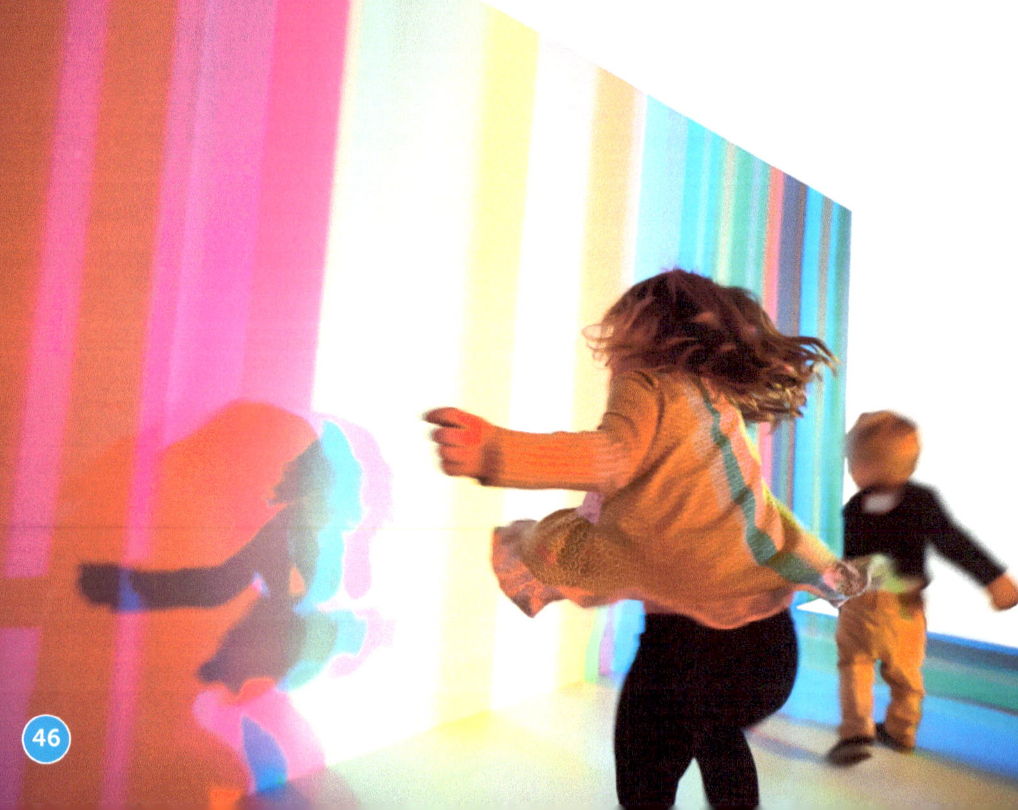

Anne Fullenkamp

(Exhibits Director since 2016)

A good Tough Art piece is something that presents a new idea in a way that is accessible to kids and adults without compromising the artist's point of view or aesthetic. We always hope that artists come away from the residency with an artwork they are proud to include in their portfolio.

Penny Lodge

The vision has to come from the artist. We have to accept that. There are often fun concepts that, as it turns out, don't have more to them and aren't able to sustain visitors' interest. There are other pieces that function throughout the three months but aren't really fun. Other work starts out looking kind of cool but doesn't last because it can't hold up to sustained interaction. There are multiple ways to succeed, and there are multiple ways to fail. The Museum is willing to experiment and accept the failures that naturally arise, and I love that.

Lacey Murray

I started the job with the attitude that everything has to work and be fantastic. I had to learn to be okay with it truly being an experiment. We have some Tough Art pieces that have been up for ten years. That is amazing. Others make it from September until the Thanksgiving holiday when we have a surge of visitors. I've learned to go in with more reasonable expectations because we're working with artists that have likely never made interactive artworks for

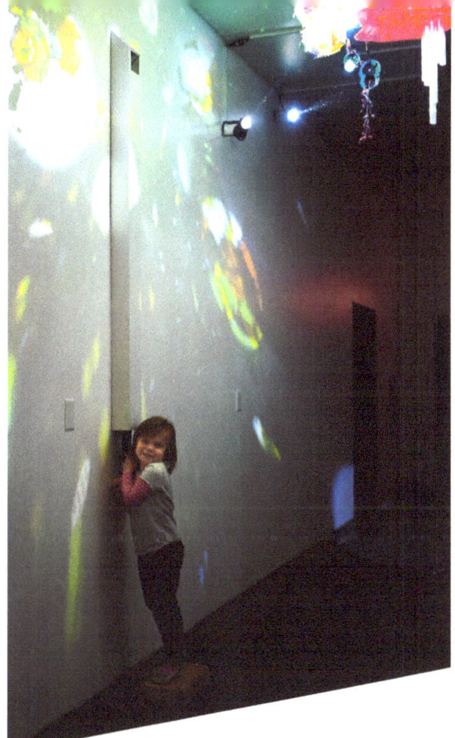

the public before. For the Museum to get one interactive work that works for our venue from the residency is an accomplishment.

Jane Werner

The most successful art pieces are the ones that make you stop and question your model of the world. And make you go, *I never thought of it that way* or *I might have to think differently about this value that I've held onto for so long.*

43: *Nimbus Drum* (Shohei Katayama, 2017)
44: *Shy Lights* (Charles Sowers, 2015)
45: *Fissure and Quake*
(Jesse Kauppila and Dakotah Konicek, 2014)
46: *Prism Palace* (Lindsay Packer, 2014)
47: *Moon, Shine* (Ann Tarantino, 2015)

Jenna Boyles

SPACE SHEEP

Scaling Up

For about a week I had been testing ideas for outer-space themed interactive sculptures in the Museum, and then, talking on the phone with my mom, she jokingly suggested that I make a "space sheep." When I got off the phone, I drew a sketch and realized it was actually a great idea.

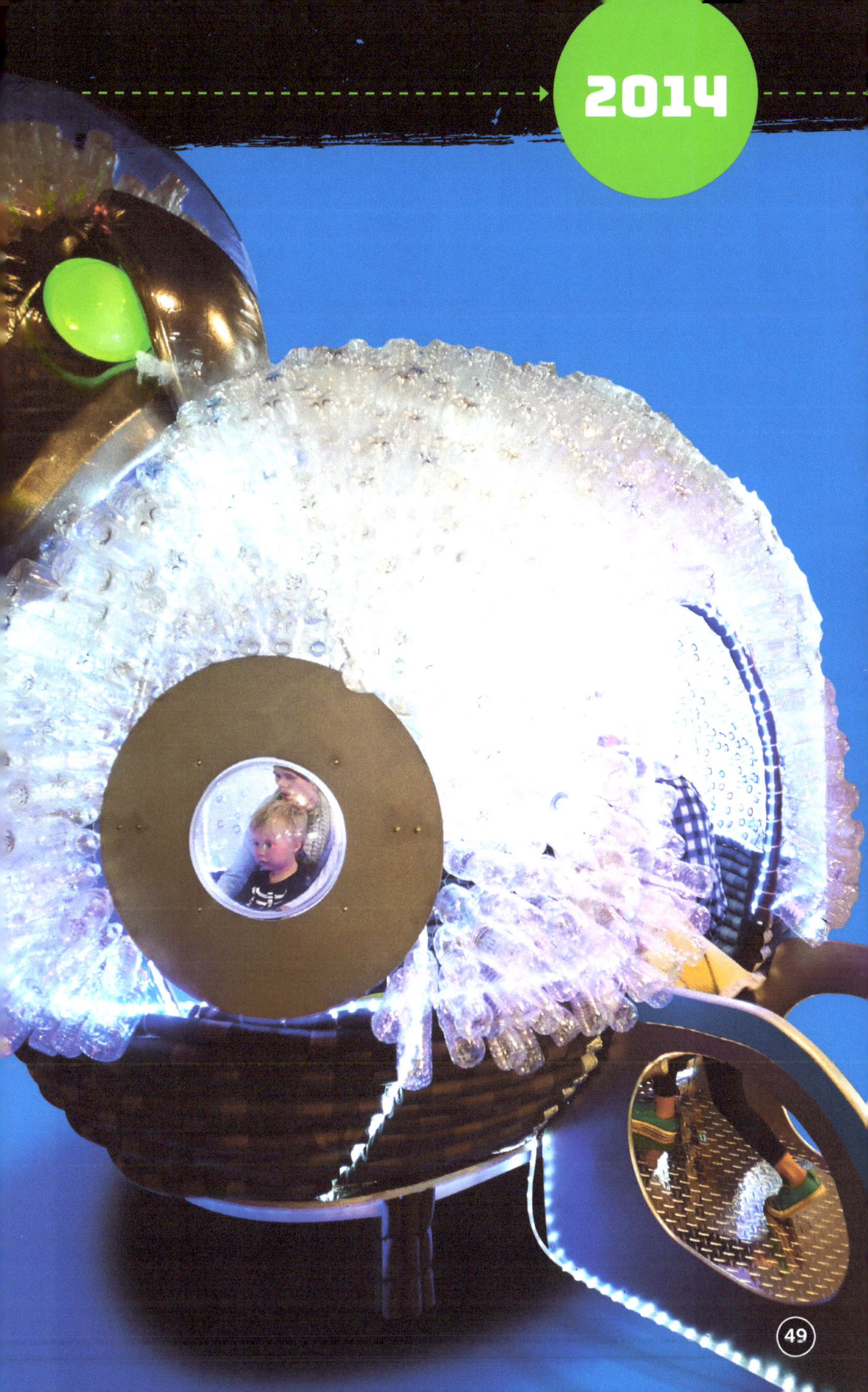
2014
49

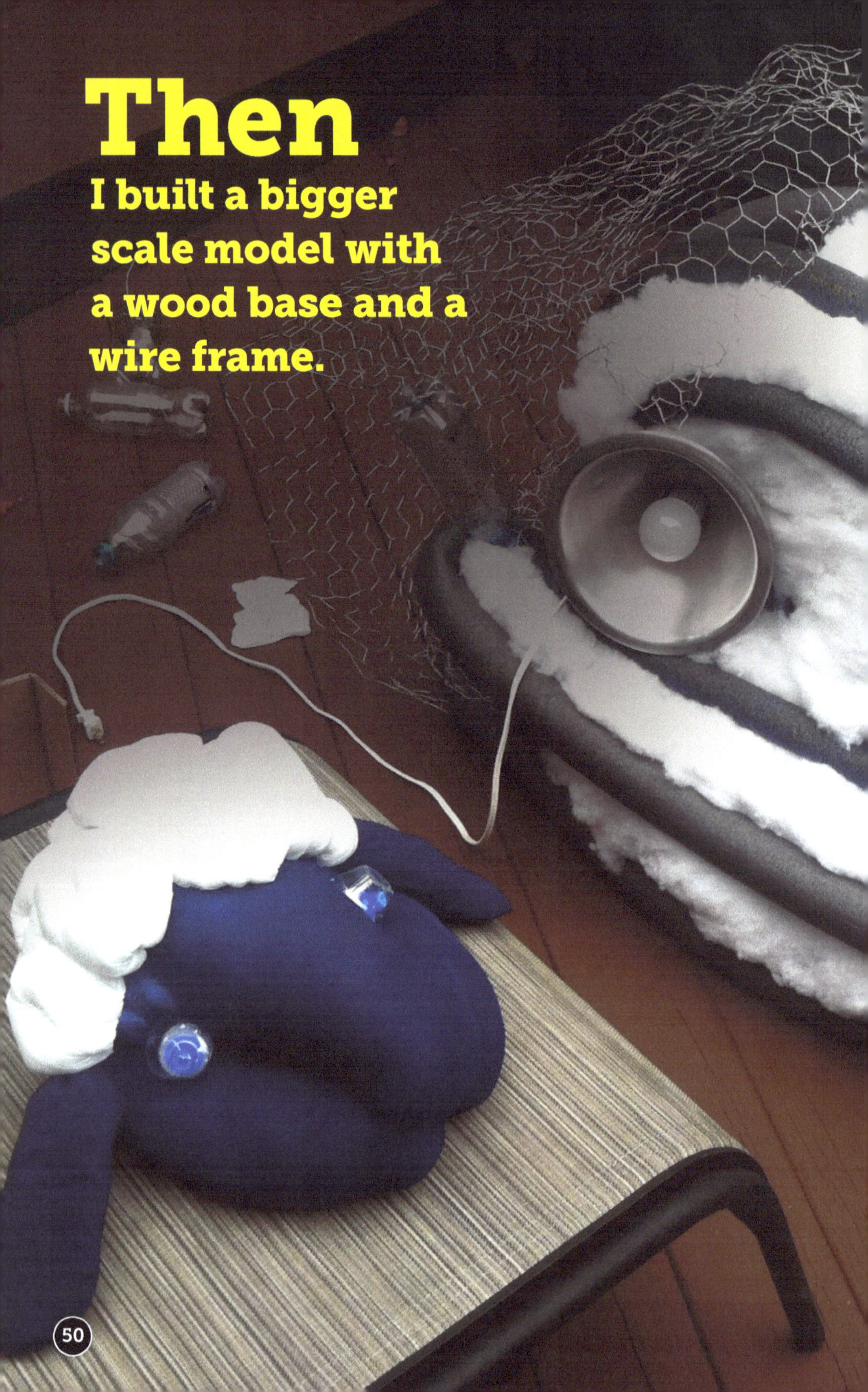

Then
I built a bigger
scale model with
a wood base and a
wire frame.
50

The first prototype of *Space Sheep* was a spaceship-flying game on a laptop with a control board made from a soft fabric, which I tested with visitors.

I also built a very small model using a pint sized milk carton, which helped me understand what the larger sheep might look like in terms of its entryway and controls. Then I built a bigger scale model with a wood base and a wire frame.

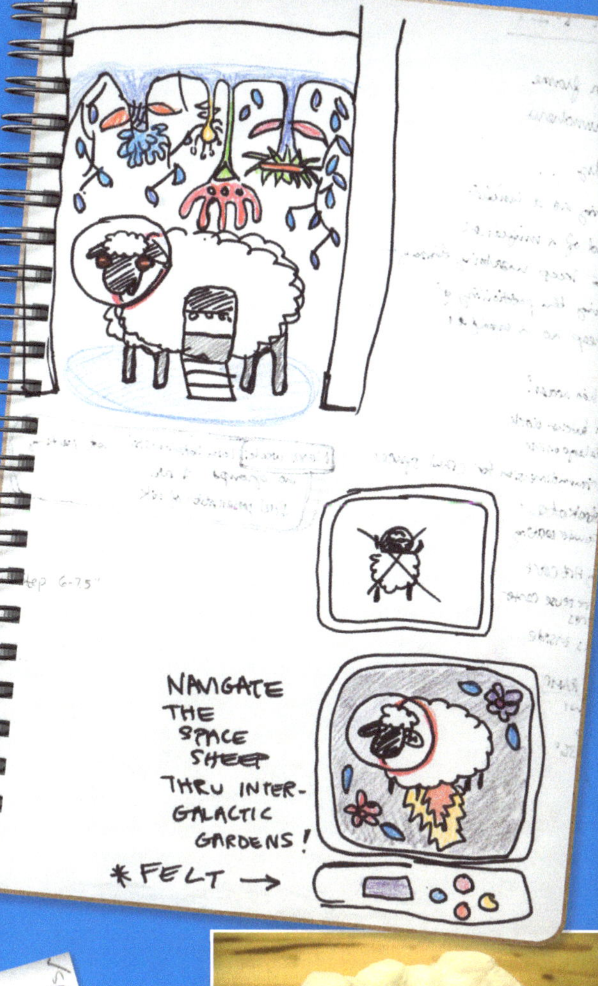

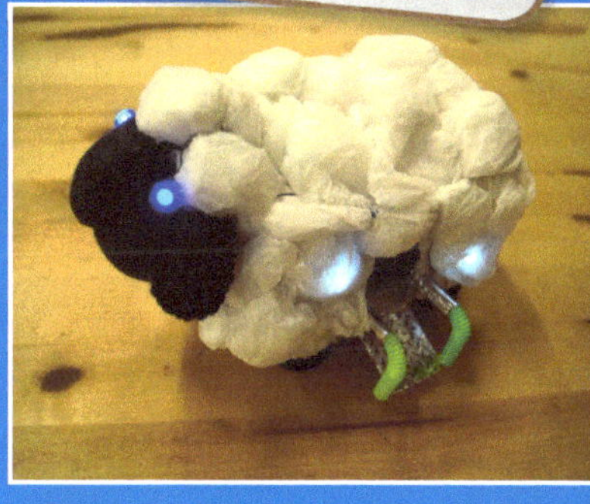

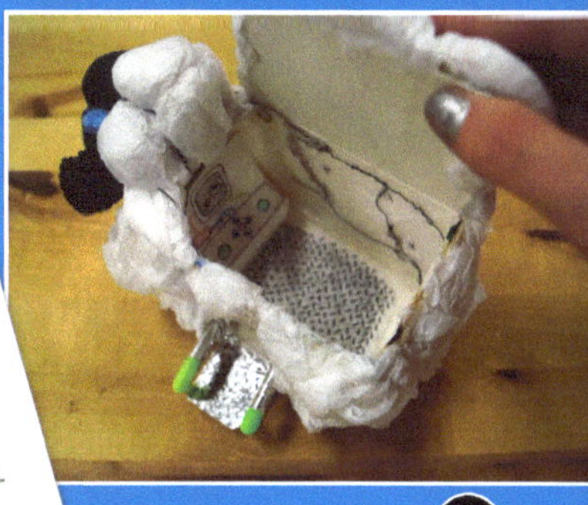

I made a separate model of the head to figure out how I'd construct it. Deciding to make the eyes from lamp fixtures helped determine the head's size. I ordered a very big, clear, inflatable ball for the space suit helmet, and my plan was to use a lawn ornament blower fan to keep it inflated. I cut the ball to fit the sheep head inside and then made sure the seam was sealed securely. It actually worked! I had never done anything like that before. This project was definitely the most ambitious thing I had worked on at that point.

— the artist, Jenna Boyles

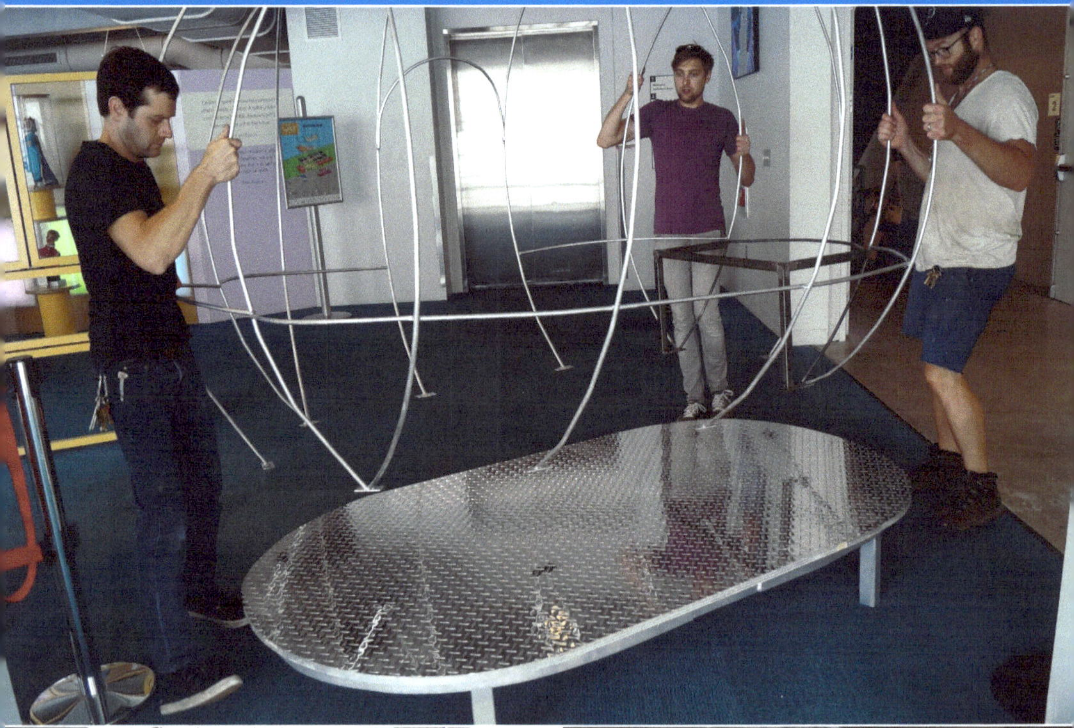

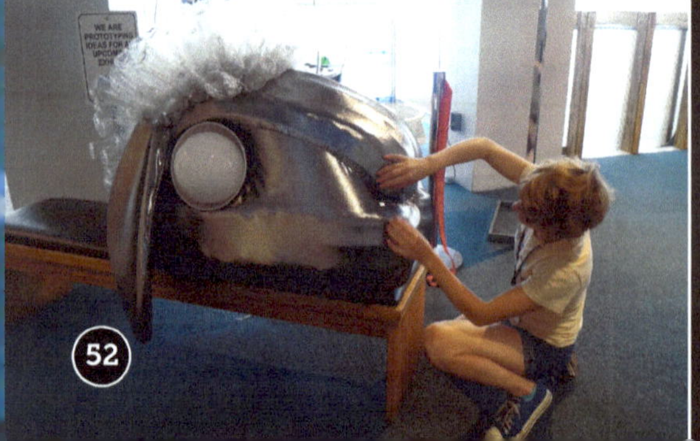

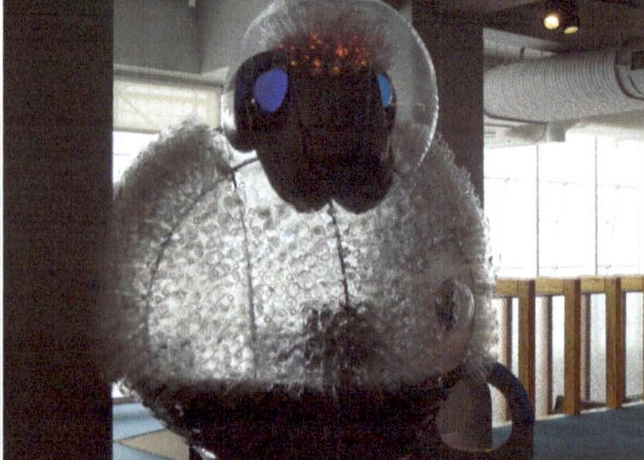

HOW TO TOUGH ART

Ten Lessons Learned

1 Clarify Your Goals

The first question to ask is: Why do you want to host an artist in residence program? What do you hope to get out of the experience and, more importantly, what will children and families get from it? Once you know *why*, then you can begin thinking about *how*. Are you open to any type of media (2D or 3D works; digital)? Do you have specific content themes to address or educational objectives? Are you looking to build a collection or focus on programming for visitor experience? Knowing the audience will be key. For example, artist residencies intending to create installations accessible to children can easily drift toward catering to adult/traditional audiences during the production process, so keeping everyone focused on the target audience is important. Hone in on the residency's goals by focusing on your organization's mission; this approach will help staff and artists keep the audience in mind during the process.

2 Identify Your Resources

How much time, treasure, and talent can you dedicate to the residency? Do you have space for the artists to work at the museum or nearby? Does your staff have time to guide artists through the process? How much space do you have to exhibit the finished artworks and for how long? How much money do you have available to support the project? Make sure your resources match your ambitions. This residency is yours to define, so set the parameters based on what is achievable and realistic, especially in the first year.

2a Determine Your Budget

The Tough Art budget has ranged from as little as $1,000 to as much as $50,000. The artists are paid a stipend and given a materials budget; the Museum covers travel expenses and other administrative costs. While stipends and other expenses have varied depending on how many artists are participating, we keep the materials budget to $2,500–$3,500 per project for the full residency. By limiting the materials budget, everyone can stay focused on quick, creative solutions.

Don't underestimate the value of things you might have on hand like scrap materials or broken equipment. Scavenging through discarded piles of materials may turn up a treasure trove of valuable tools and materials for an artist.

3 Start Small and Stay Local

Once you know your resources, you can begin to structure the residency. How many artists can participate? How long will the residency last? Beginning with two or three artists from your community is a realistic way to start, especially if this is your first time hosting a residency. Working with local artists simplifies management of the program because you won't have to account for travel and lodging needs. Also, local artists might be more familiar with the culture of your museum and audience. Starting small will also help your staff integrate new responsibilities into their routines.

4 Create a Cohort Culture

While the thought of hosting more than one artist seems daunting, a group of two or more will be able to learn from one another as they go through the process together. Regularly scheduled group critiques allow artists to receive feedback from each other and staff. Ideally, the artists will push one another in their artistic process. This replicates the art school experience by combining independent and group work. Creating a culture where they can look to each other for advice—and not just rely on museum staff—can help them create artworks that are distinct from your museum's exhibition style.

Organize small social gatherings like a field trip to a local cultural event or a happy hour so the artists and staff can get to know each other outside of the workday setting

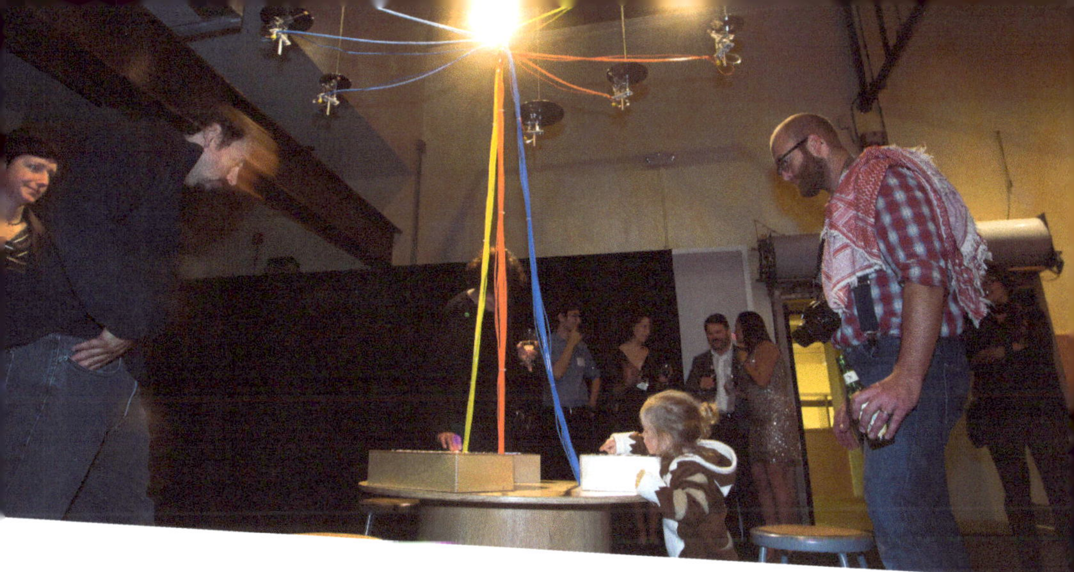

5   Choose Participants Wisely

Artists should have a proven track record of delivering complet-
ed artworks, regardless of their level of experience. They should
be able to demonstrate their ability to take an artwork from con-
ception to completion, on time and within budget. With this in
mind, you can determine the mix of skills you want to bring to the
cohort, considering the capacity of your staff and facilities. Don't
necessarily pick artists whose work is obviously "for children." The
point of Tough Art is to expand everyone's thinking about what
art in a museum focused on a specialized audience can be.

tip: *Be cautious of artists who propose artworks "for
children" that are vastly different from the rest of their
portfolio. We want artists to explore their authentic
artistic practices while also respecting children as an
audience on par with adults.*

6   Make Time to be a Mentor

Your staff members need to be available to artists throughout the
residency. As in all true collaborations, good communication and
understanding of each other's goals are key factors for success. Staff
will have to balance their residency responsibilities with their daily
work, so build the residency into the departmental/museum schedule.
Treating the residency activities like other important operational tasks
tells the staff and artists that your organization has made the program
a priority. The end results will be better when everyone feels supported.

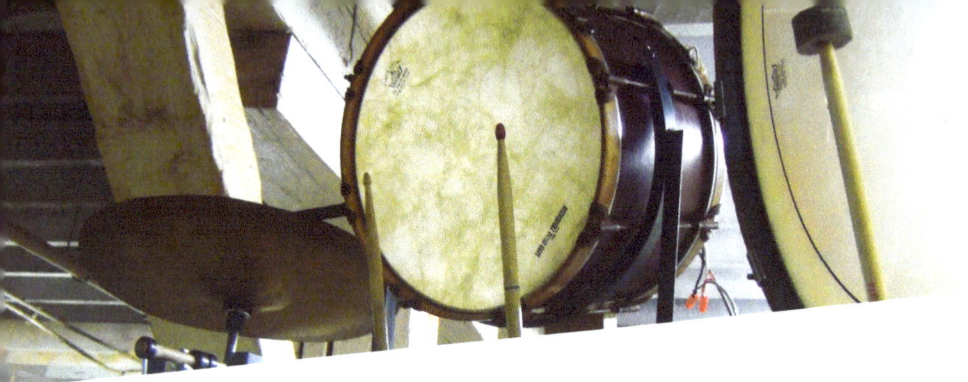

7 Prototype, Prototype, Prototype

For artwork to succeed in the context of an interactive environment, iterative prototyping is a must. This is the time for artists to get to know their audience, see their idea in your museum's context, and engage directly with kids before their artwork is finalized. Many artists will not have had this opportunity before, so organizing introductory prototyping practice runs as exercises at the beginning of the residency will help artists understand the goals of prototyping and the staff's expectations. Giving artists time to experiment with small projects before they really get into their artwork can be a welcome opportunity, easing any anxiety by clarifying their skills set and identifying where they may need help. This is also a chance for staff to offer some coaching in technical skills, material use, and other basics—outside of the critique of their artwork. The prototyping process provides an opportunity for artists to field questions that they might not have considered alone in their studio. And prototyping can and should apply to the entire process, even down to the language and placement of signs.

8 Accept Failure as Part of the Process

We love the saying "you can't fail a museum." Unlike what we experience in other parts of our world, children's museums are places where misfires and mistakes are not only tolerated, but celebrated as part of the creative process, leading to inspiration and innovation. Taking risks with the full understanding that results are not guaranteed is a key part of the experimental process we encourage in the Tough Art residency. Rather than expecting every artist to create an engaging, robust original interactive work, expect them to learn about new creative processes and new potential experiences for your visitors.

9 Celebrate, Celebrate, Celebrate

We celebrate the conclusion of each residency with an exhibition opening party. Unlike many art gallery openings, our Tough Art parties feel more like a graduation party, with artists inviting friends and families not only to see their work, but to meet their fellow artists and the Museum staff who participated in their intensive journey. Over time, the guest list has expanded to include Museum supporters and other arts professionals. Ultimately, not all of the art will prove "tough enough," so taking the time to acknowledge both the artists and staff is more meaningful than a traditional critique. Make sure you are allocating time to play, have fun, and celebrate the participants.

10 Experiment, Learn, and Grow

In the fifteen years of Tough Art, there have been fifteen versions of the residency. Each year is a little different than the year before. From the Museum's perspective, we try to build on what's working and discard what's not, from administrative tasks to advertising to exhibition design. Most importantly, each year we try to select artists who are notably different from their predecessors, challenging ourselves to bring a variety of ideas and skills to the Museum.

tip: *Change things up regularly and resist the urge to play it safe. By making deliberate and strategic changes, you can build a more sustainable and interesting program over time.*

55: *Syncopated Rhythm* (Jeremy Boyle and Kevin Clancy, 2012)
56: *Drum Machine* (Matt Barton, 2007)
57: Prototype for *Urchin Searchin Sound* (Arvid Tomayko and H. Gene Thompson, 2017)

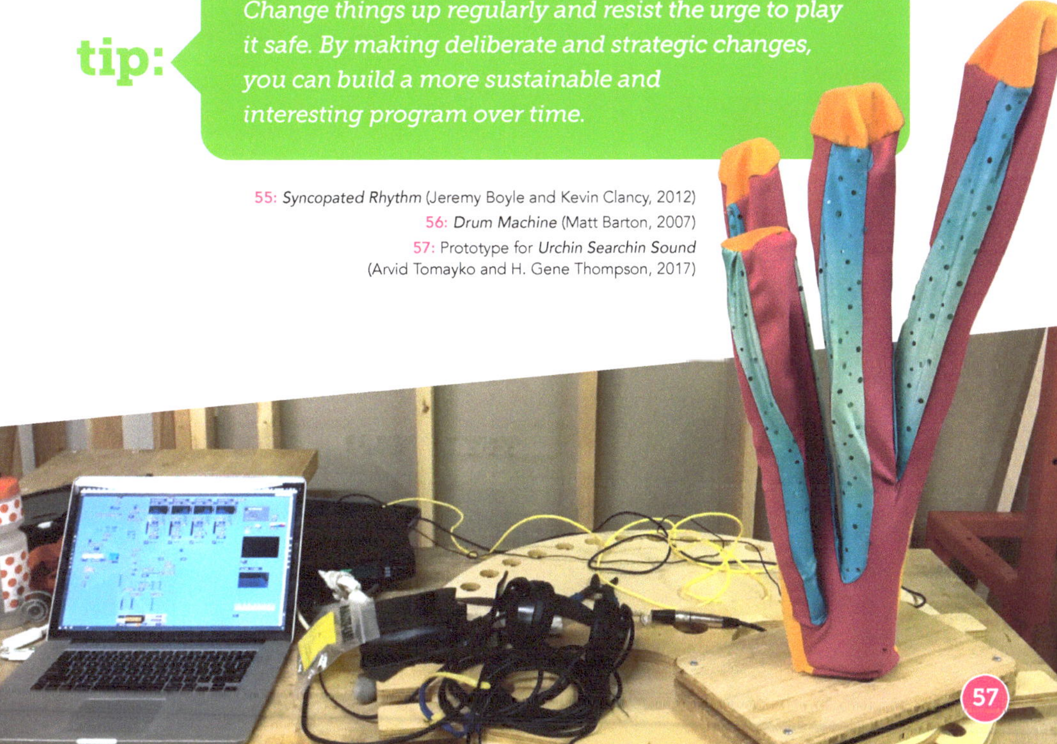

TOUGH ART CALENDAR

While the residency takes place in the summer, program activities occur year round.

Fall Preparation

Planning for the residency begins by reflecting on the previous year. This helps us make decisions about the upcoming budget, the scope of work, and parameters like the timeline, location, and number of artists. The official call for artists is prepared to be publicized through the Museum's website, university art departments, online artist residency listings, art associations, individuals' social networks, and community spaces that may cater to artists and makers.

December / January

The call for artists goes live with a "Request for Qualifications," which solicits the artist's bio, examples of previous work, professional references, and a short letter of interest. There is also an option to propose a potential Tough Art piece, but this is not required.

Behind the Scenes: This option came about five years into the program to encourage artists to start thinking about the residency more specifically during the application process. We don't expect applicants to hold onto that first idea, but it offers insight into their artistic process

February

Museum staff visits local artists' studios, gallery openings and college campuses, actively recruiting applicants. This outreach extends to neighborhood gallery crawls, community centers, and coffee shops to reach a wide range of applicants.

March

Prospective applicants are invited to visit the Museum to see the space and ask us questions. This offers applicants more context and helps them decide if this residency is a good fit. The call is closed at the end of the month, and applications are received and organized by the project manager.

April

The Museum's exhibits team narrows down the applicants to a select group of finalists who are then reviewed and discussed by the core staff who will be working directly with the artists. When reviewing the applications, we take into consideration the artist's capabilities and skills as exhibited through their previous work, their potential for a productive collaboration, and their capability of creative experimentation with the Museum's unique resources. Some applicants are asked to participate in a virtual interview to ensure their candidacy is assessed thoroughly. Selected artists are contacted and start their preparations for spending the summer months at the Museum.

May

Museum staff prepare for the new cohort, arranging for workspaces, lining up mentors, and organizing exhibit galleries in anticipation for new prototypes and artworks. The project manager makes travel and lodging arrangements for Tough Artists from outside the local area, as necessary

June

Tough Art begins with Orientation Week!—a crash course in what Tough Art means at the Museum. This starts with an intensive introduction to the Museum, the staff, our specific prototyping process, visitor behavior, the gallery spaces, and the workshop. The artists are shown many examples of interactive experiences in the Museum, illustrating different ways to create durable and appealing interactive artworks. They are also given a brief history of Tough Art, including lessons learned from the past and specific goals for their residency.

July

Artists develop their concepts and build prototypes to test at the Museum with young visitors. Weekly meetings with Museum staff help track progress and problem solve.

By the end of the month, the artists will have selected a location in the Museum for their artwork, confirmed their budget, and created a clear plan for building their final piece. This requires that they find the right balance between their aesthetic intention and the often-exuberant instincts of the Children's Museum visitors.

Behind the Scenes: Many Tough Artists find this phase of the project personally and professionally challenging. Cohort and Museum staff support is often essential to artists while navigating these unfamiliar challenges.

August

Artists' final work plans are approved and Museum staff will start making any necessary changes to exhibition spaces to accommodate the new works. In August, the artists are usually working in their studios or the Museum workshop on the final build and spending less time on the floor with visitors. Staff will make frequent visits to the artists' workspaces, checking on their progress, answering questions, and assisting with fabrication, if needed. The final installation schedules will also be confirmed as some artists need more assistance and time with installation than others. Signs accompanying the artworks are drafted, edited, and sent to print. Promotion materials are prepared, including artist statements.

September

The artworks are installed around Labor Day in preparation for the opening party (mid-September) that marks the conclusion of the residency and the launch of the exhibition. This event is a high point for the artists and staff after the intensity of their summer work. Tough Art alumni, other artists, arts professionals, and friends and family are invited to meet the artists and join in the celebration. The next day, the pieces are officially on display at the Museum and promoted through the Museum's media channels

Through January

The aim is for Tough Art installations to be on display in the exhibit spaces until the following January. Artists agree to be available for troubleshooting and repair during this period, working closely with Museum staff on maintenance plans when necessary. The reality is that some artworks are more robust than others;

maintenance or repair challenges may necessitate removing some artworks from the public space sooner than planned. But that's part of the process.

Following the Temporary Installation

The residency is structured to create temporary works of art. The temporary scope also supports the Museum's goal to provide new experiences for visitors, which necessitates regularly changing the contents of the galleries. As a result, most of the Tough Art installations are deinstalled in January and stored for a possible future re-installation. Some of the artworks are left in place for an additional three months or longer, depending on the location, condition, or content of the artwork. The biggest determining factor is how well a piece works at the Museum as a more permanent exhibit: Does it function reliably and without constant upkeep? Does it represent a media or include an experience that is unique? More importantly, do visitors like it and find it intriguing? All of these factors go into determining how long the piece is on view.

Behind the Scenes: All artworks created during Tough Art are owned by the Museum. The artist holds intellectual ownership of the concept and is free to develop something similar or adapt the work for other projects and institutions.

Below: *Bubble Device #5* (Nicholas Hanna, 2016)

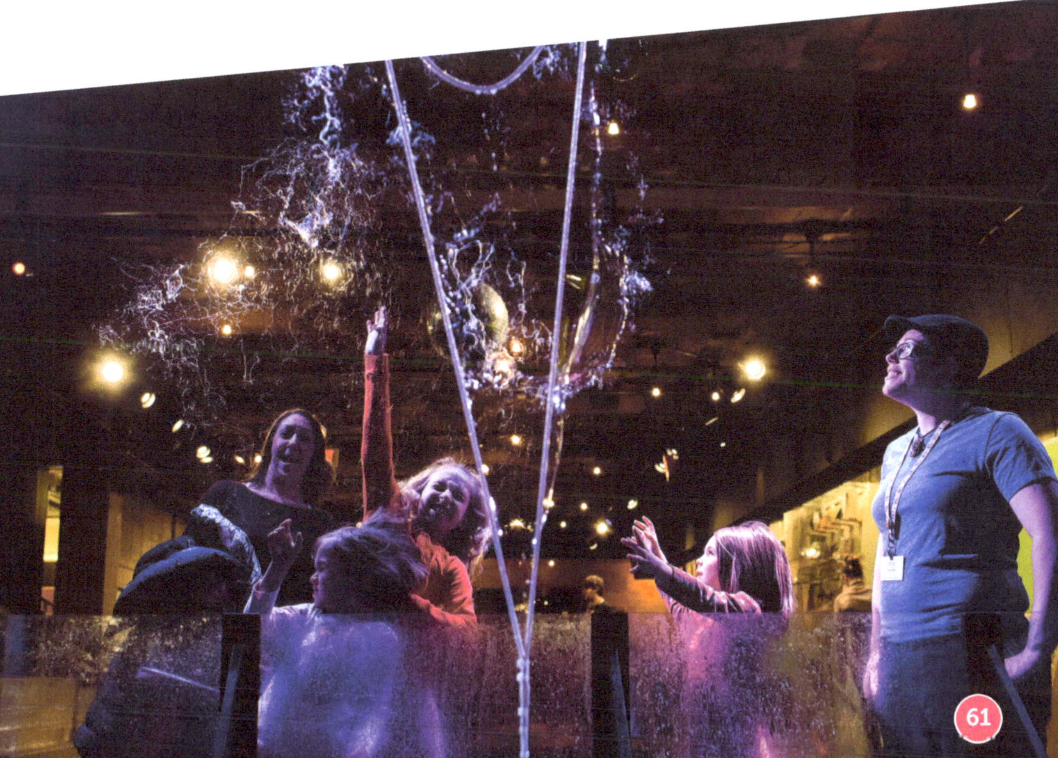

Eunice Choi

TOMATO MEDLEY

Ideas and Practice

The project idea Eunice settled on involved silicone-casting many tomatoes with different styles, or "personalities." These included characters such as "Rapunzel Tomato" with a long braid, or "Yoga Tomato" bent into a backbend stretch. She created a beautiful sketch of about one hundred different tomatoes and then narrowed her selection down to around twenty-five to use in the final installation.

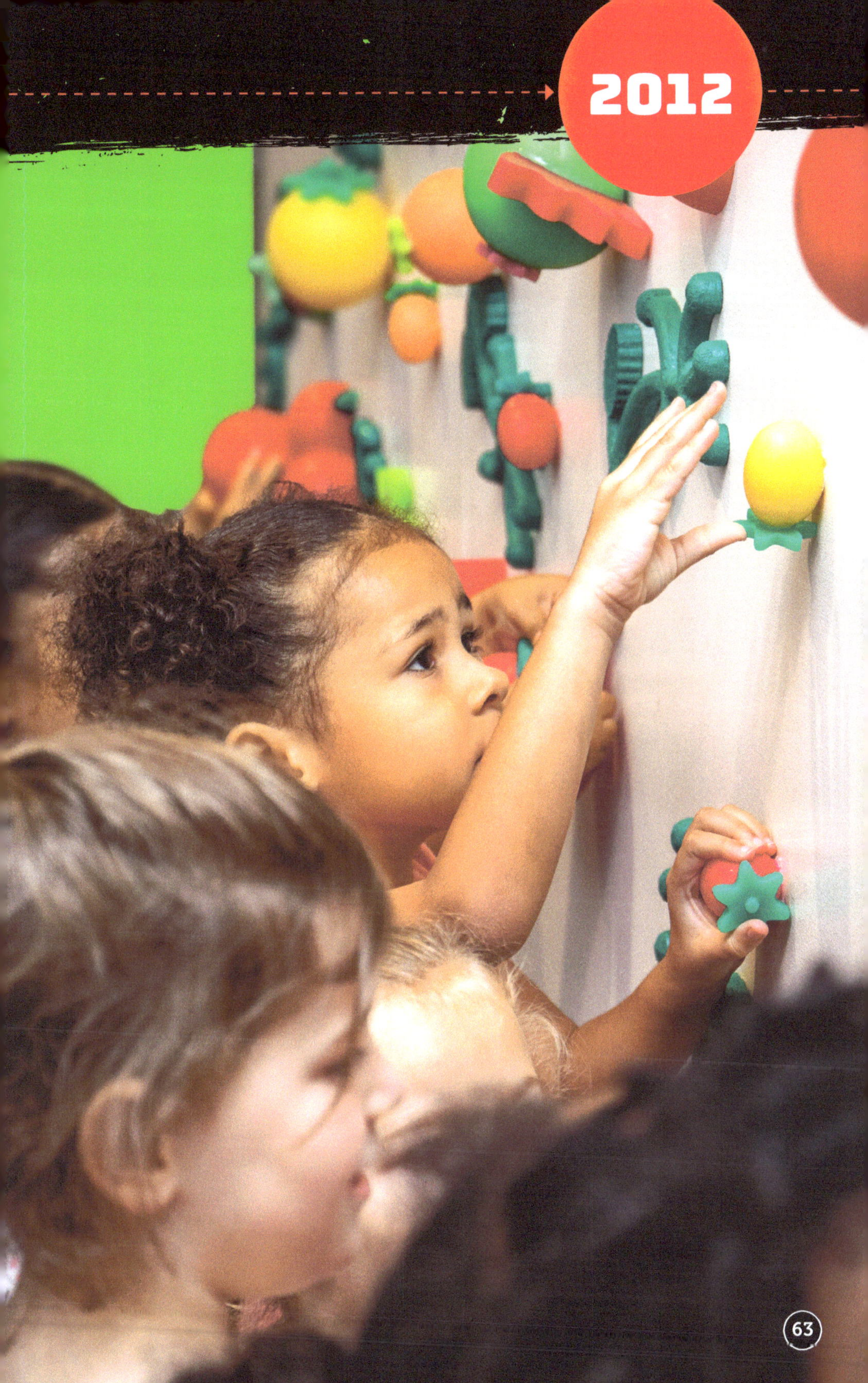

2012

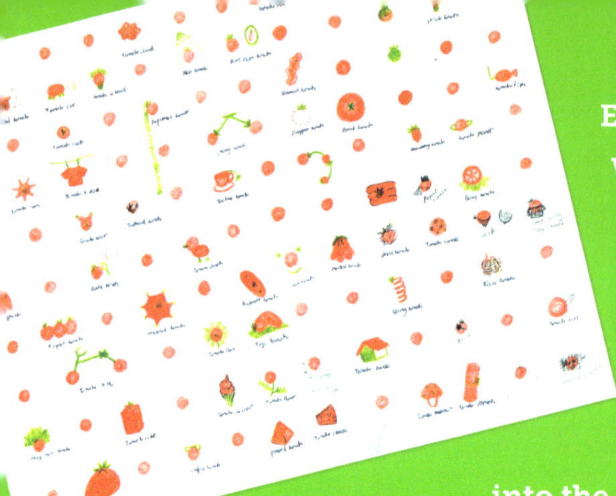

Eunice had experience working with silicone, but the challenge was making it durable enough for children's interaction. She created molds of these forms and later poured silicone into the forms to create the final tomatoes. Working with our exhibit designers and technicians, Eunice secured the tomatoes to a large, wall-mounted wooden panel. Another layer of interaction she created was a spinning wheel that featured digitally drawn images of some of the tomatoes, challenging visitors to spin the wheel and find the tomato it landed on.

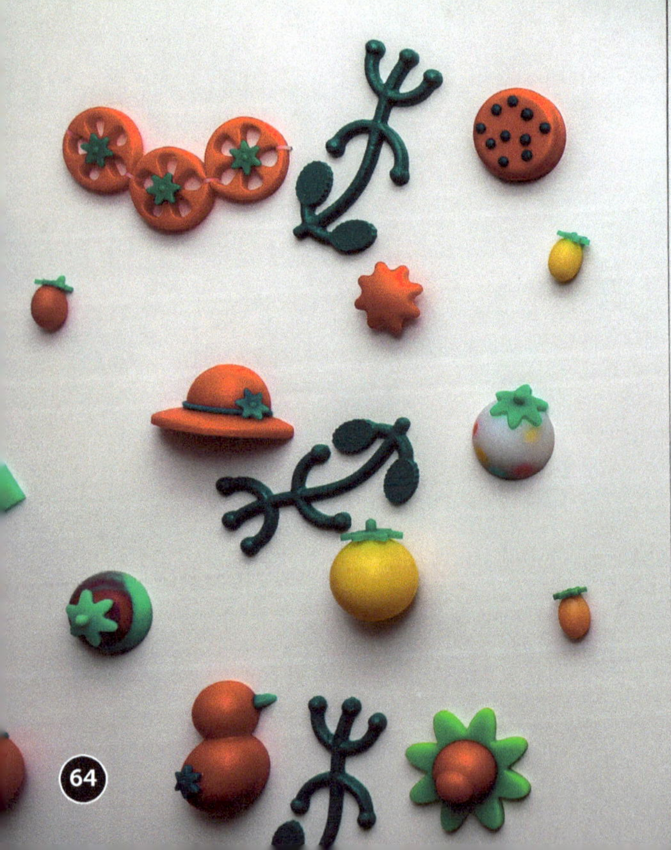

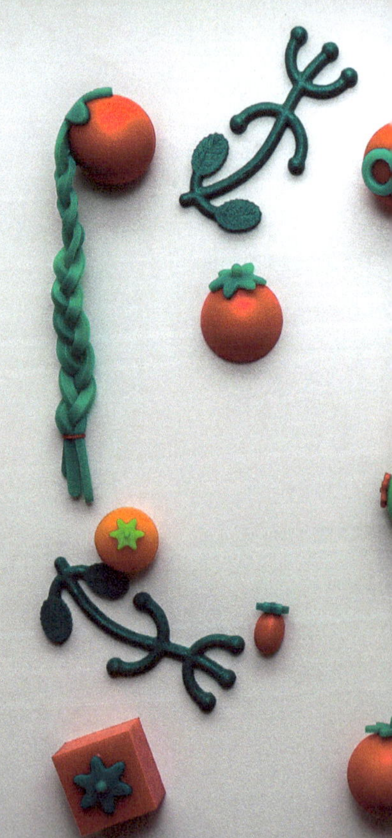

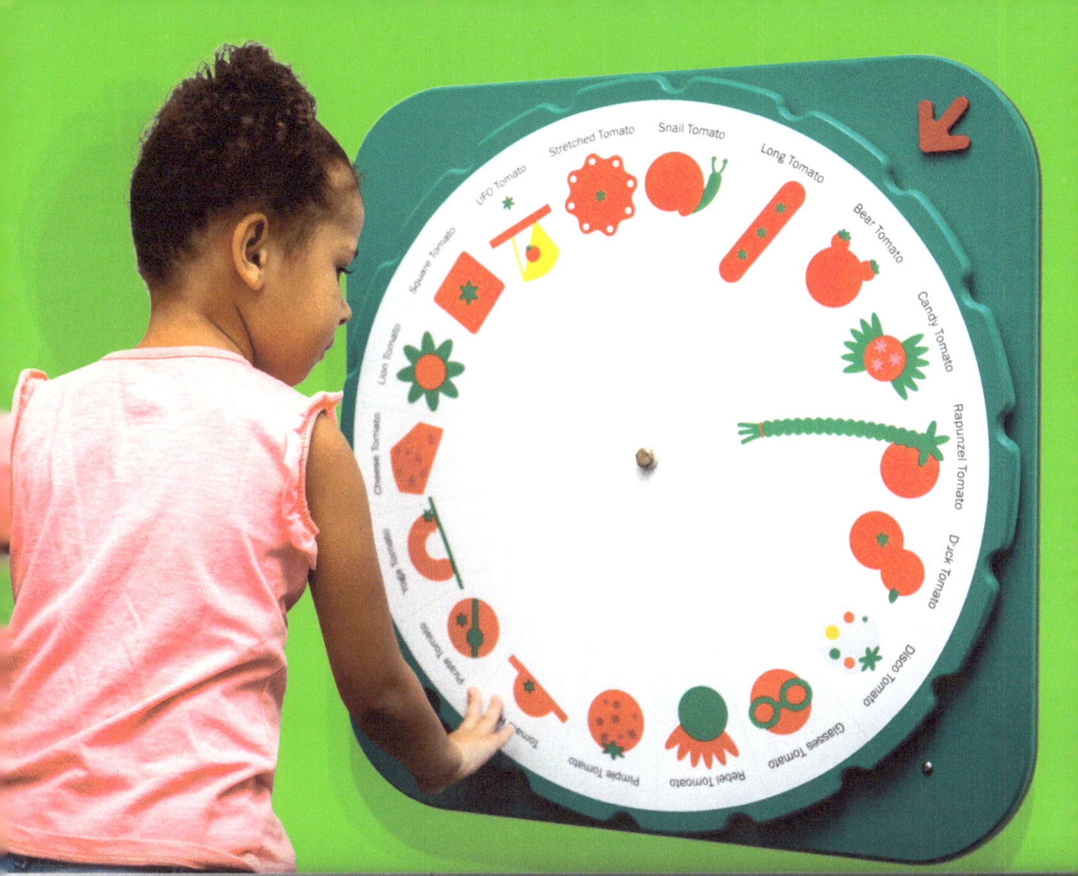

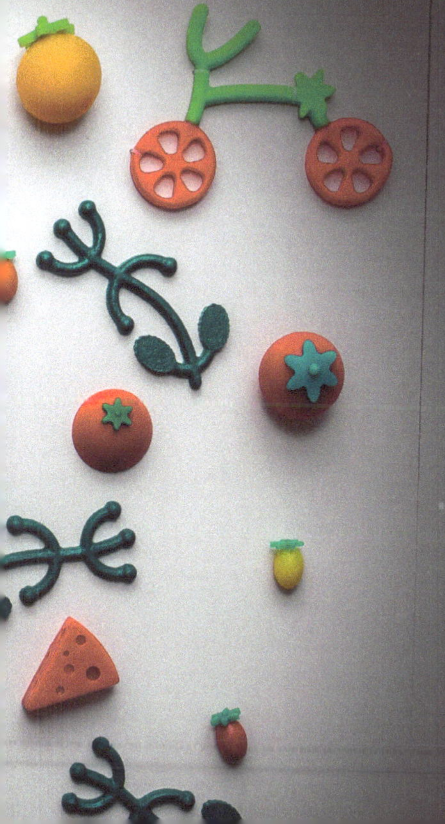

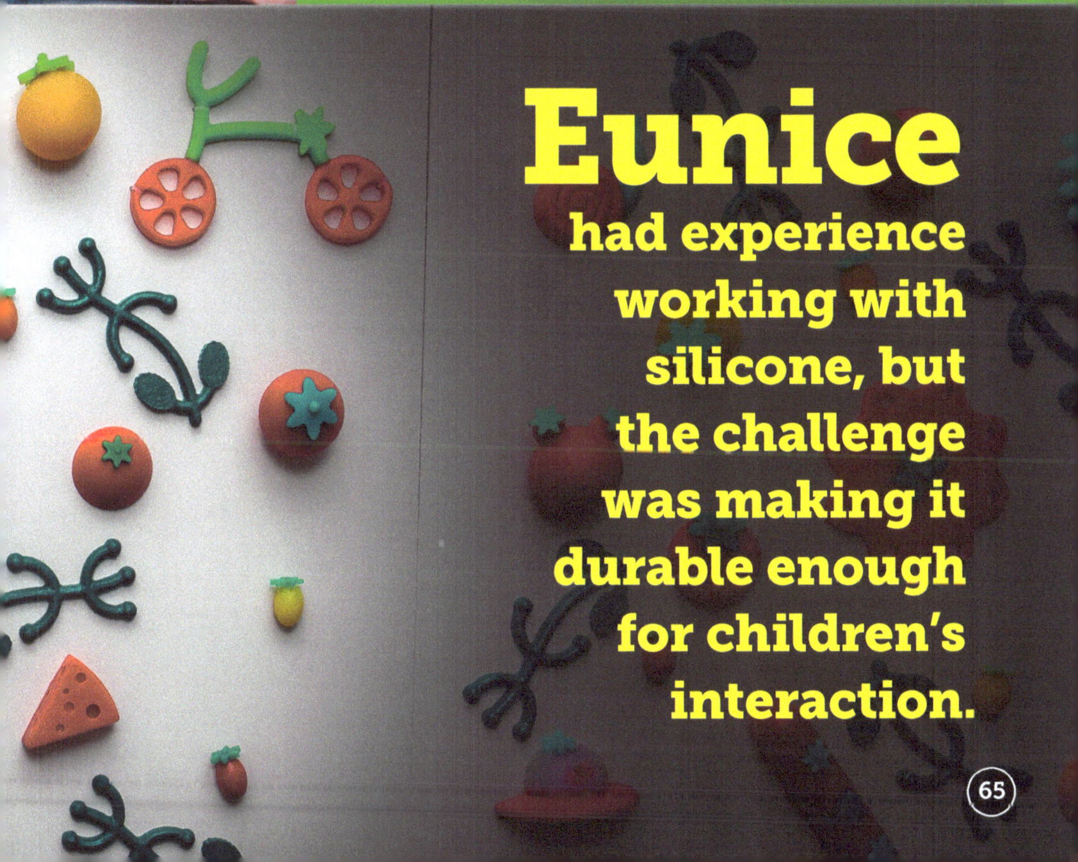

Eunice

had experience working with silicone, but the challenge was making it durable enough for children's interaction.

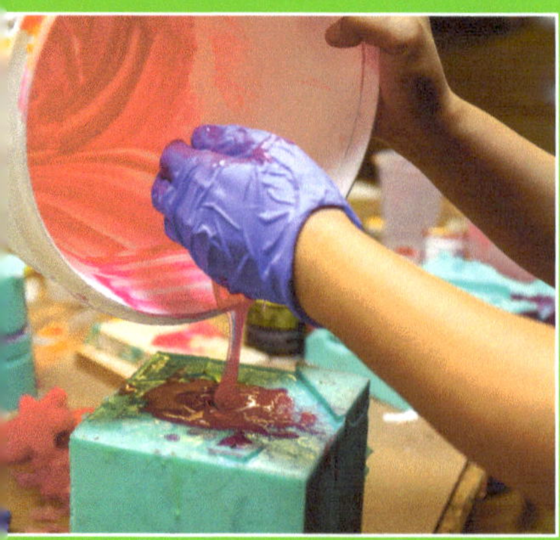

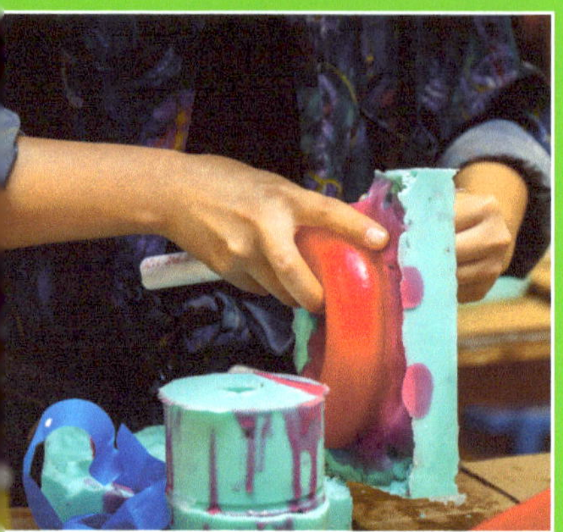

Eunice was a dedicated, extremely hard worker who spent countless nights at our shop working on her artwork. Her piece proved to be a beautiful and intriguing work of art, which unfortunately could not stand up to kids' degree of interaction. Many of the attachments were ripped off during play, and our efforts to repair and amend the piece did not suffice.

A couple years later, though, we transformed the piece into a tabletop and relocated it to The Nursery, which caters to our youngest visitors (birth to age four). The piece enjoyed a second life in this less busy location.

—*Lacey Murray*

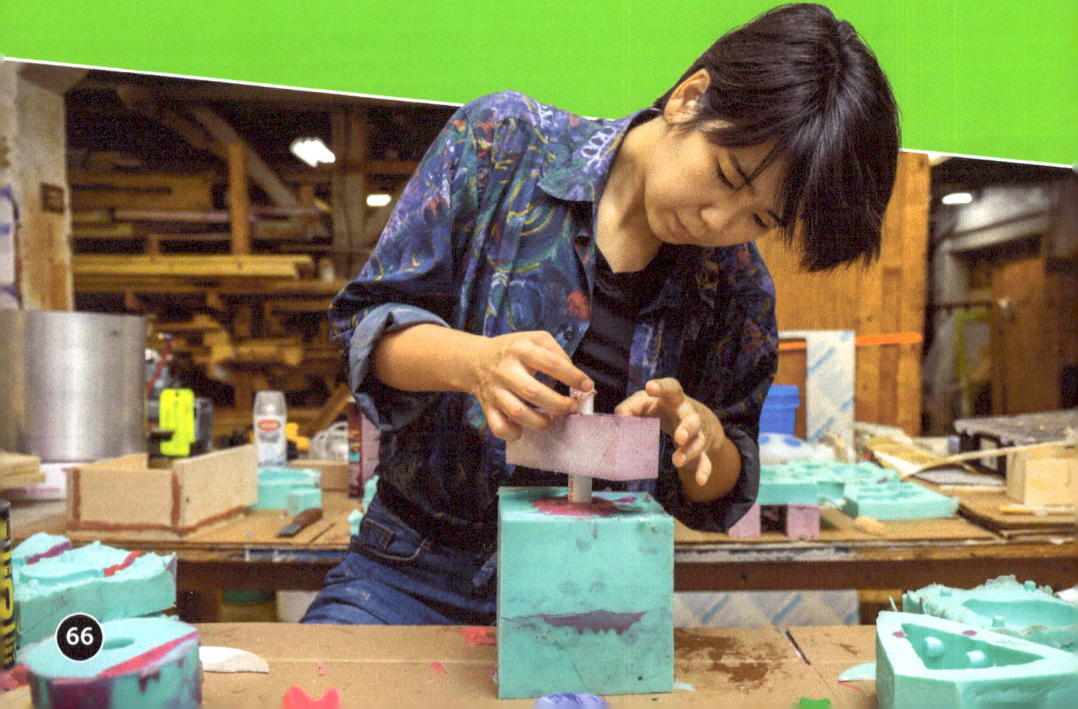

THE FUTURE OF TOUGH ART

Fifteen Years, Hundreds of Prototypes, More than Seventy Artists and Original Artworks, and What's Next

Children's Museum of Pittsburgh

has proven that it is possible to support artists in creating original interactive artworks that can withstand the exuberant curiosity of young visitors. In short, the Tough Art residency program *works*. What started as a bold experiment—without precedent in the children's museum community—has become core to the Museum's culture.

One by one, cohort by cohort, the residency has provided artists with a unique opportunity to learn specialized skills, adapt their artwork through our version of robust prototyping, and bring to bear what they have learned in the process. A number of Tough Artists have gone on to residencies at other children's museums and many have expanded their reach to work with other youth-serving institutions such as schools and libraries. Some alumni continue their relationship with the Children's Museum through creating components for traveling exhibits, serving as mentors for new Tough Artists, or participating as teaching artists at the Museum.

Internally the program has provided staff with frequent opportunities to work with artists, become familiar with different art practices, and exchange ideas with new creative partners. Staff look forward to getting to know and collaborate with the new Tough Artists each summer. The ongoing dialogue and problem-solving process between the staff and artists encourages everyone to think differently about their own work. For example, collaborating with Tough Artists has introduced staff to the use of open-source programmable Arduinos, new kinds of casting materials like silicone, and innovative forms of interactivity. These learning experiences function as real-world professional development for staff with each artist bringing their unique skills, methods, and challenges to the table.

Tough Art started as an experiment, and that spirit has continued over these fifteen years. In 2020, the COVID pandemic put this exper-

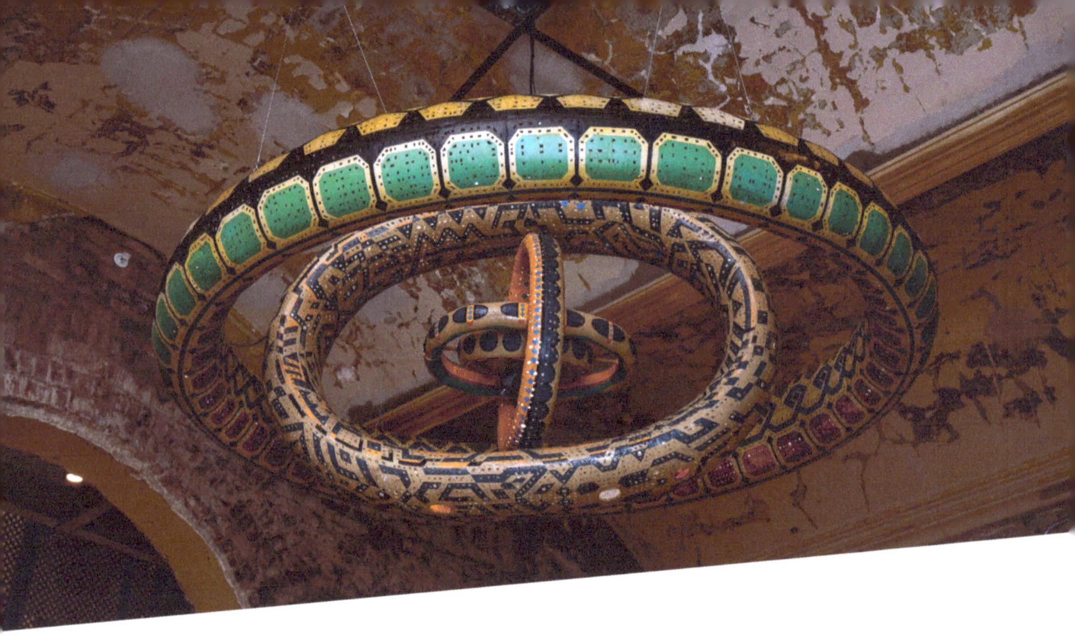

imental approach to the test; due to Museum closures, the staff was forced to radically rethink the format of the residency. Program Manager Lacey Murray quickly developed a new version—*Tough Art @Home*—in which artists shared unique creative art activities online, making the art and artists accessible to children confined to their homes. Along with online art instruction, artists provided downloadable PDFs, with creative activities people could do on their own, like artist Jeff Repko's Marvelous Machine project that details how to build your own industrial machine sculpture.

The reimagined *@Home* version offered a life-line for families, teachers, and kids who were desperate for new and meaningful activities to do at home that would also help them stay connected to familiar places and people. Unexpectedly, *Tough Art@ Home* reached people previously unfamiliar with the Museum or Tough Art, connecting the Museum with new audiences all around the world. The program was so successful that the Museum commissioned a second cohort of artists in 2021 for another year of *Tough Art @Home*. Additionally, in the spring of 2021, Tough Art alum Owen Lowery created a collection of outdoor sculptures accompanied by mobile phone-based audio stories, yet another example of how the Museum adapted the idea of Tough Art in response to the pandemic. In this case, the Tough Art was placed outside so that it was accessible, even while the facility was still closed.

Tough Art has inspired other internal variations, such as solo in-person residencies at the Museum. In 2019–2020, former Tough Artists Scott Garner (2013) and Neil Mendoza (2018) were Technologists-in-Residence for six-month residencies, each creating new works at the Museum. As alumni of the program, they brought their Tough Art experience to the new residency as they created suitably durable and

working in and with different neighborhoods in Pittsburgh. Local community representatives would participate in the prototyping process, providing feedback to the artists to enable site-specific artworks that are "tough enough" for specific communities, much like the artists do at the Museum.

And, if Tough Art works in Pittsburgh, why couldn't it work in other cities around the world? A reach goal is to build the Tough Art model into a world-wide community of practice, connecting artists and youth focused museums to create meaningful and robust artworks all around the world. This could take the form of profes-

And, if Tough Art works in Pittsburgh, why couldn't it work in other cities around the world?

intriguing technology-based artworks, both of which are now part of the Museum's permanent collection. In 2022, Dutch based hi-tech fashion designer and innovator Anouk Wipprecht is designing and fabricating a new work while also prototyping new ways to deliver workshops for children as a way to make her work more accessible to broader audiences.

As the in-person Tough Art residency has resumed post-pandemic, and we look forward, we ask ourselves: *what's next?* One goal is to expand Tough Art beyond the Museum campus. This could take the form of a community-based residency with Tough Artists

sional development programs for artists and arts administrators, as well as emphasizing the adaptability of the program to local resources and venues. Formatted like a Tough Art "boot camp," these sessions could embody the hands-on, learn-by-doing approach that the Museum employs with the Tough Artists themselves.

Another idea is to work directly with museums across the country and abroad by initiating Tough Artist and mentor exchanges with those museums. The residency process, artist alumni, and diverse range of successful artworks are all assets for public art planners and prospective funders. Looking at all of these possible offshoots collectively, the process and results of Tough Art provide valuable reference points for public art projects that aim to appeal to a wide range of people in informal settings, well beyond children's museums or formal arts organizations.

As we look forward, we aim to think more expansively about the Tough Art residency as a model for project development beyond exhibits and across disciplines in the Museum. One of the biggest benefits of the program has been the relationships between the artists and staff. As temporary coworkers in an atmosphere based on experimentation, this collaboration fosters an ability to share novel perspectives and challenge conventional ideas with freedom and collegiality; the adage "you can't fail a museum" underlies this summer residency. What if a similar approach was applied to other disciplines at the Museum, like education, marketing, or even finance and administration? Would those teams feel reinvigorated like the exhibits team does? Would they acquire new skills from guest collaborators? Would they see their daily work in a different way, even temporarily, that would help them innovate their practice? Is there a way to apply an artist residency model to other disciplines that create a culture of innovation and camaraderie?

Dissemination of Tough Art know-how is an ongoing effort. Our staff has presented at museum conferences and written articles describing the program from both the artists and staff perspectives. Pittsburgh staff enthusiastically offer realistic advice to colleagues within the children's museum community, as informal word-of-mouth inspires

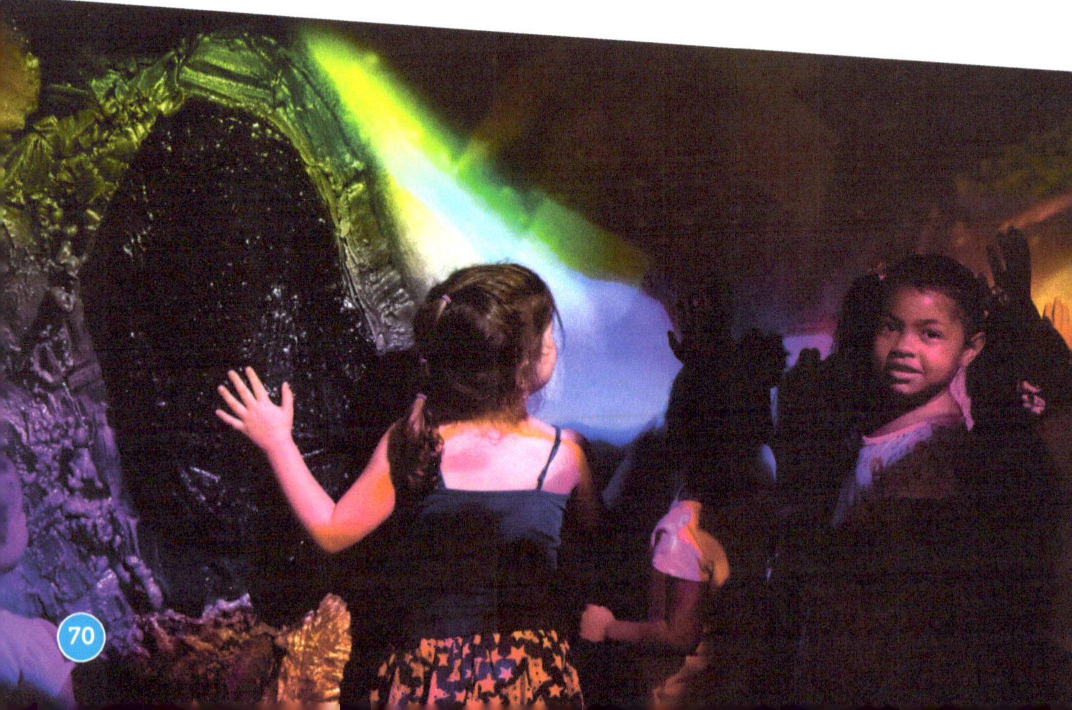

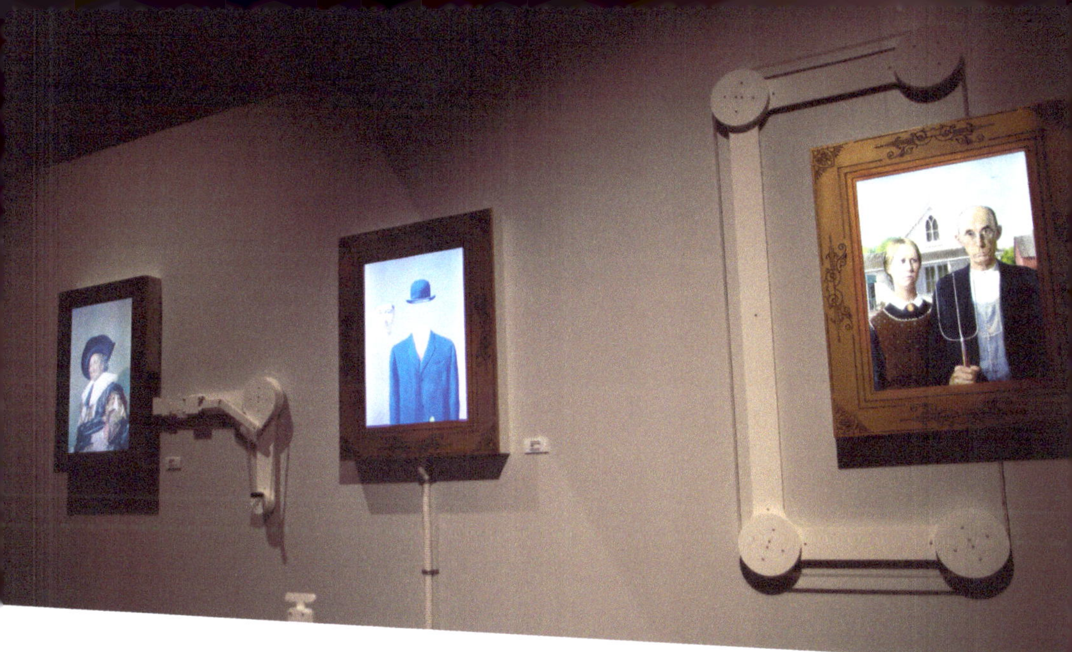

like-minded efforts. Looking to our Museum as a role model, some children's museums have developed similar artist in residence programs. The Providence Children's Museum, Amazeum (Arkansas), and The New Children's Museum (San Diego) have all commissioned work from or collaborated with artists to create hands-on experiences for their visitors.

Though Tough Art has continuously evolved over the years, the one consistent goal has been to authentically engage young visitors. Kids are the arbiters of success or failure in this environment, and their responses are often unpredictable. Tough Art is both a model that can be adapted for other children's museums (or museums who want to attract younger audiences) and a source of insight that can help museum professionals and artists think beyond the typically simplified and sentimental aesthetic of "art for children." Contemporary art for young visitors can and should be dynamic and inspiring. Children in art museums should be welcomed, not feared. While there may be no tougher audience for art than these young visitors, this audience is also candid in their expression of genuine curiosity, appreciation, and wonder.

68: *Compound Ringship* (Ryder Henry, 2019)
70: *Cosmic Geometry* (Owen Lowery, 2019)
71: *Mechanical Masterpieces* (Neil Mendoza, 2018)

AFTERWORD

Advice to Artists from Ned Kahn,
Artist and Frequent Children's Museum Collaborator

A children's museum is a super tough environment,

and to make something that will endure is a challenge. With kids playing, anything that's breakable gets broken. At the Exploratorium, I often witnessed crazy stuff happening when visitors played with interactive exhibits. You might already have spent time carefully building and engineering your prototype, and you would be totally confident, thinking, *Okay, this is totally solid and visitors are going to do x, y, z.* Then you put it out in the public exhibition space and stand back to watch the first few energetic visitor encounters when they do unexpected things. All you can think is "Oh, my God" before you quickly pick it up and bring it back to the workshop to make changes.

I remember some of the artists in residence at the Exploratorium would show up with really interesting ideas, but they weren't prepared for the hands-on energy of that environment. When you think about the Museum calling the program "Tough Art", yes, it's a physically tough environment, but the program also toughens artists to interface with the real world.

I think the context of camaraderie for the Tough Art residency program is super important, too—among the artist cohorts and between artists and the Museum staff. If the approach was just to give each artist their own studio and instruct them to do their thing and tell us when you're done, it would be a failure. It's a tremendous opportunity for artists to receive lots of feedback, give constructive feedback, learn to process feedback, and understand entirely new challenges.

Many artists have had experience with group critiques from art school, when you're trying to impress teachers and trying to impress your fellow students. Maybe this is unfair, but I have the impression that sometimes the more convoluted your thinking and language, the more you con-fuse your teachers and classmates, making them think you're smart.

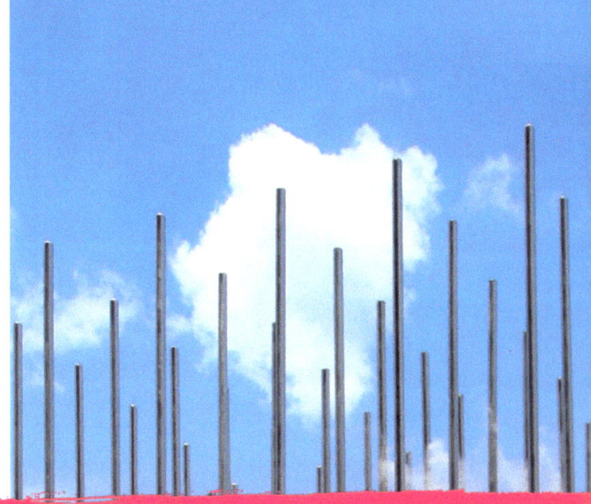

To just step back and think about what's actually there in front of you and to realize these kids are not going to know anything about the history of art is a big shift in perspective. Kids are not going to know what postmod-ernism means and they're not going to know all this gobbledygook. The challenge is to put aside your theory and abstract thinking and get into the mind of a kid. It's a huge shift of gears.

While kids will gravitate towards certain things, I have seen over and over how adult intuition, including my own, can be completely off tar-get. I remember when my daughter and son were really little, and I was working on a vibrating sand piece at the Exploratorium. The sand would move in these fascinating convection

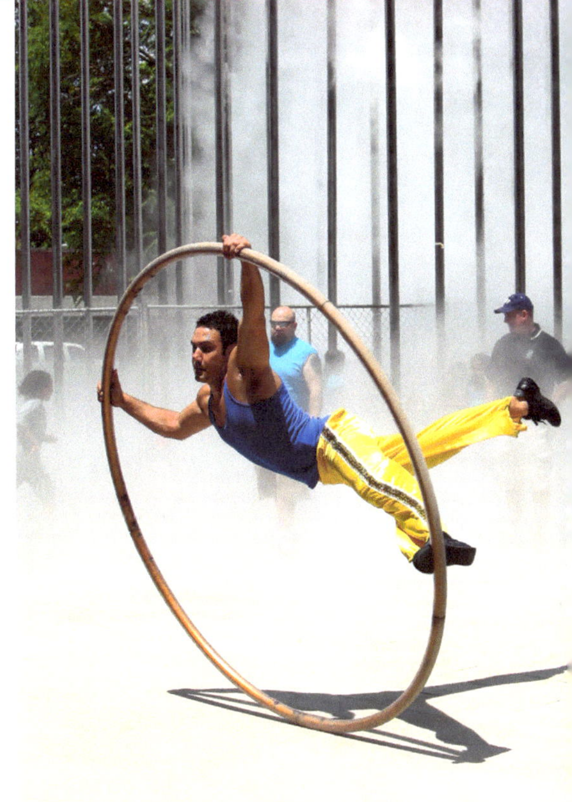

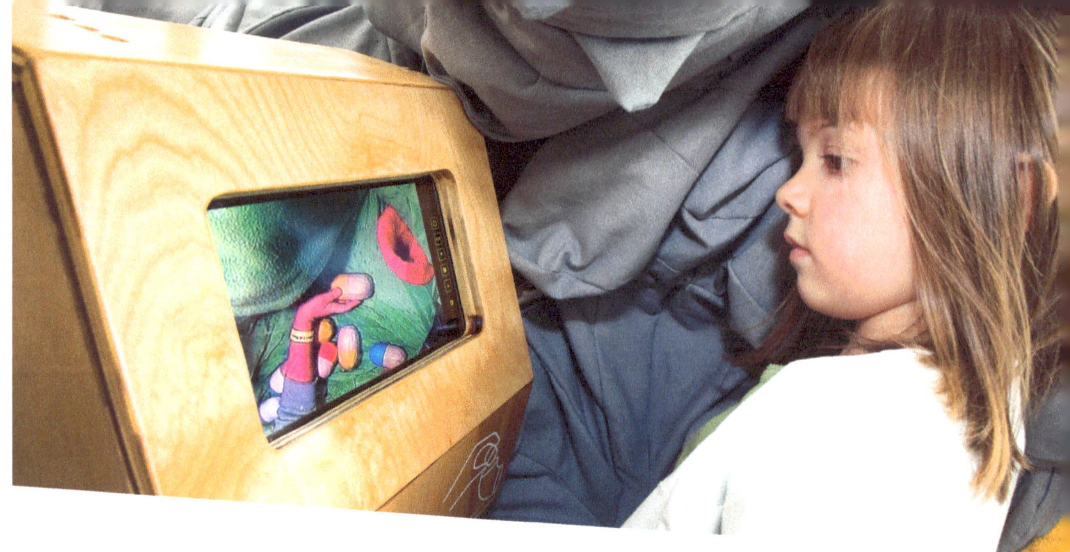

patterns in an open shallow basin so you could put your hand in and feel it moving. I thought, *Oh, they're going to love it. This is going to be so cool.* When I brought them in, they played with it for thirty seconds and then asked, *Can you turn the motor off?* They just wanted to play in the sand. The fact that this vibration motor was moving the sand bothered them. I had completely the wrong idea. My artistic jive was, *Here's nature sculpting the sand* but theirs were, *Stop the motor—we want to play with the sand.*

Many years ago, when I was still at the Exploratorium, Jane [Werner] quizzed me about the artist in residence program and what made it work. I told her that the most interesting projects were the open-ended ones. The whole idea of having open-ended prototyping and trying things out is the path to discovering something amazing. And of course, it's also a path to failing many times along the way, before arriving at an amazing discovery.

I remember going to a lecture by artist Robert Irwin, and someone asked him what gift he had that allowed him to make these amazing artworks?" He answered, "My only gift is I've always given myself complete freedom to fail." Irwin talked about how, without that freedom to fail, you're always trying to do something that you've already done, already seen, or already know is going to work. The only way you can do something new is to take risks.

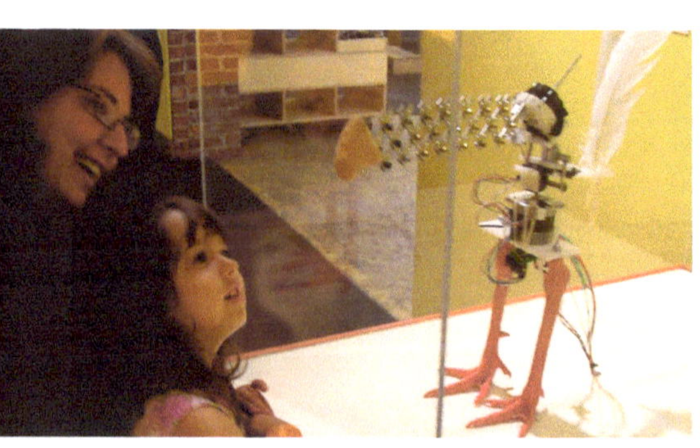

Working this way takes the stress off of having to succeed. It allows for surprises and 180-degree course corrections too. You start with one idea. and it doesn't do what you think it's going to do, so you find something else totally different. You have the freedom to follow the new path that opens in front of you.

Ned Kahn creates public art and commissions for museums and community spaces in the United States, Europe, Australia, and China. His work has been recognized with a MacArthur "Genius" award and a National Design Award. The Children's Museum commissioned Kahn to create two large outdoor sculptures,"Articulated Cloud" and "Cloud Arbor".

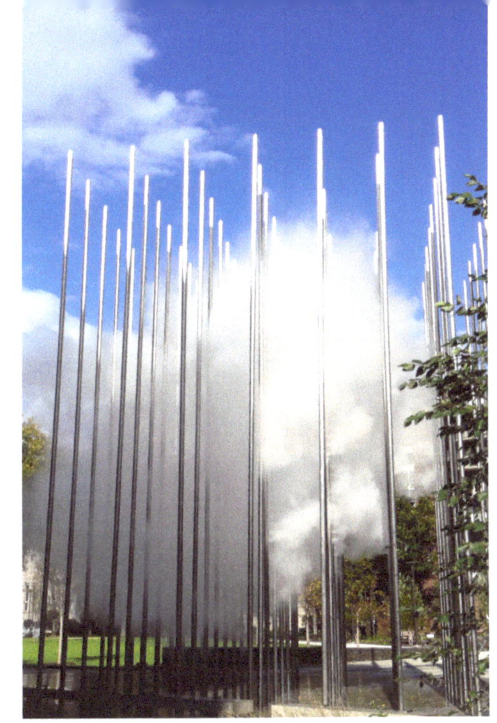

73: *Cloud Arbor* (Ned Kahn, 2015)
74: (Top) *Monstroscopy* (Isla Hansen & Luke Loeffler, 2013)
74: (Btm) *Nutnukin-Kinnutkin* (Ian Ingram 2009)
75: (Top) *Cloud Arbor* (Ned Kahn, 2015)
75: (Btm) *The Nest* (Megan Flød Johnson 2017)

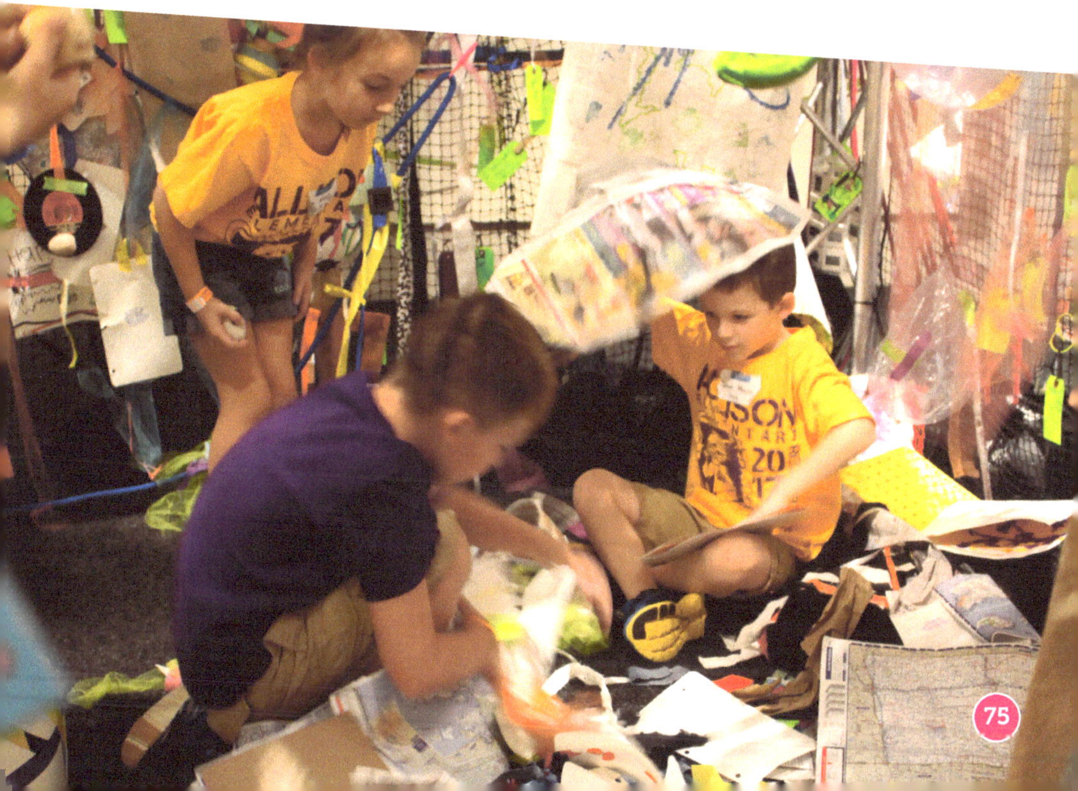

TIMELINE OF TOUGH ARTISTS

2007

Eileen Maxon	*Broadcast*
Greg Witt	*Floating Platform*
Joey Hayes	*Windy World*
Matt Barton	*Drum Machine*

2008

Ben Bigelow	*A Day in the Life of a Tree*
David Butts	*Giant*
Rick Gribenas	*An Obscured Neutral Moment #2*
Wendy Osher	*Bullies in Our Woods*

2009

Anneka Herre	*Drop Ceiling No. 3 (Dark Store)*
Ian Ingram	*Nutnukin-Kinnutkin*
Jennifer Van Winkle	*the eXpedition*
Matt Mets	*Ferrous Wheel*

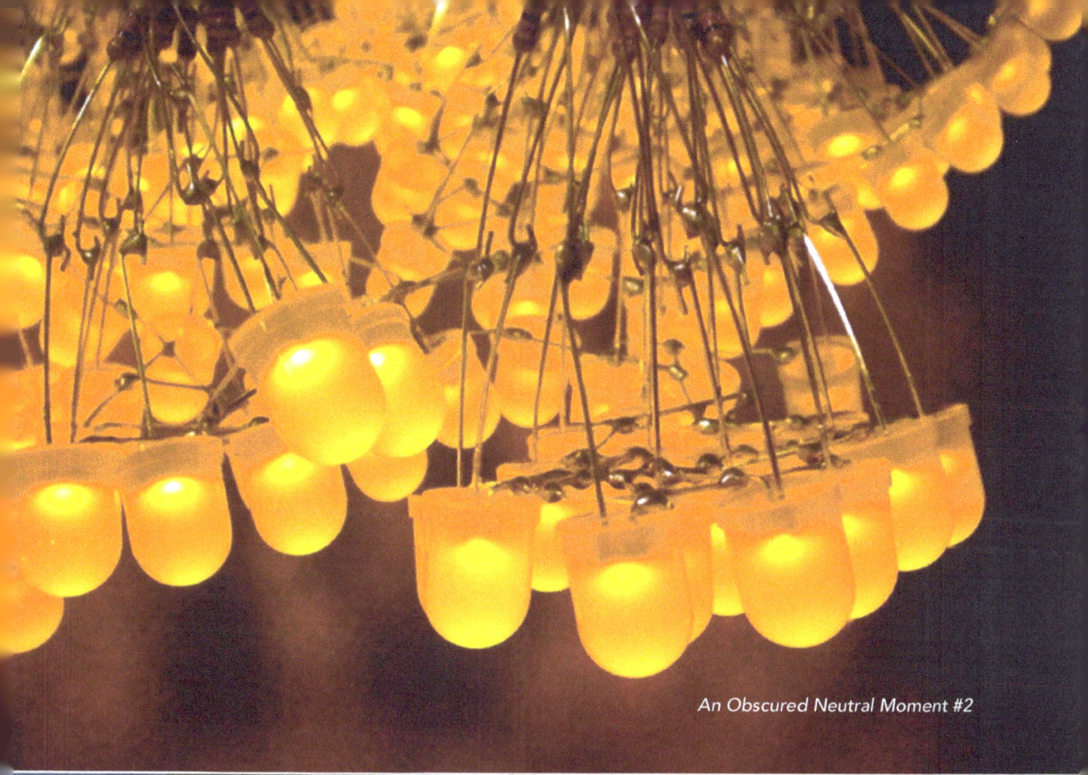

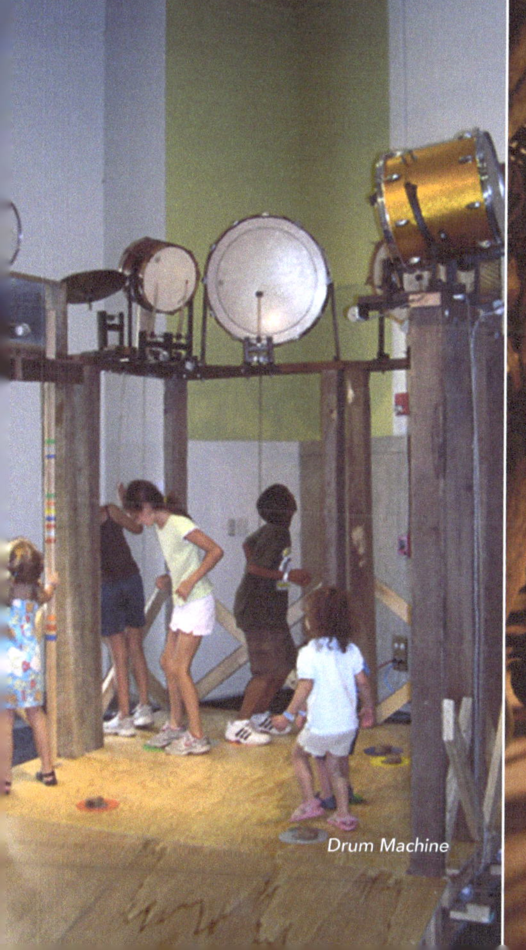

Drum Machine

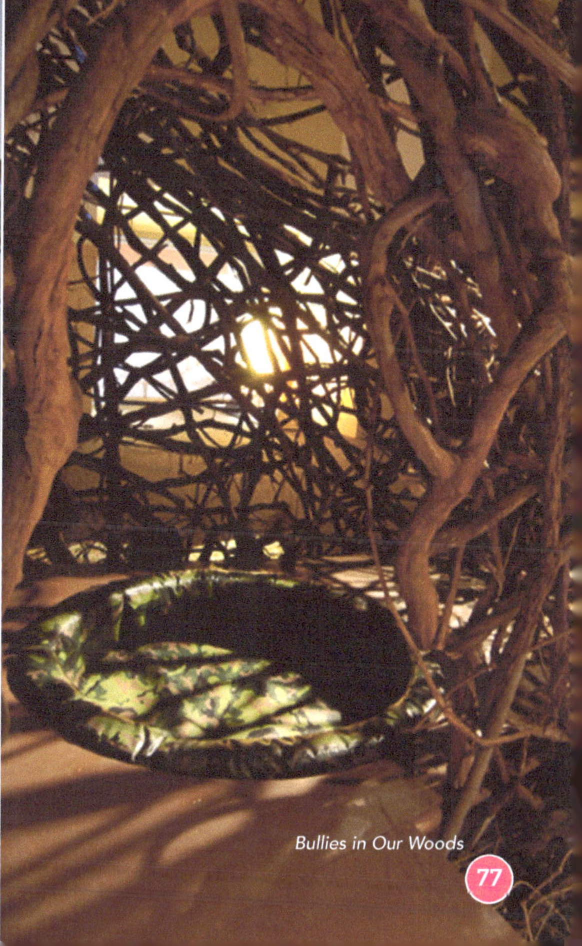

Bullies in Our Woods

An Obscured Neutral Moment #2

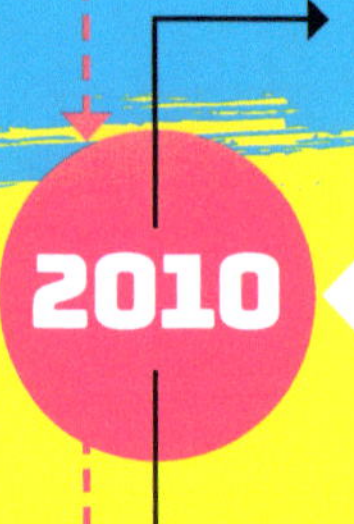

Agnes Bolt & Arthur Jones .... Temperamental Stairs

Blaine Siegel .... Aerophone

Nova Jiang .... The Beast

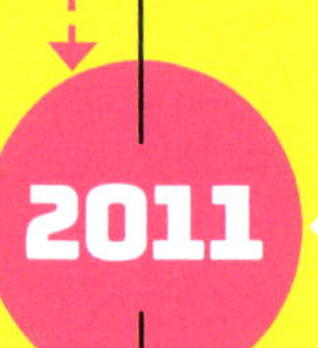

Christina Zaris .... Giant Interactive Kaleidoscope

Daniel Luchman & Jennifer Myers .... Queen Simon and The Sommeloth

Felipe Castelblanco ... The Invisible Wall

Zach Dorn .... The Honorable and Bewhiskered Herman Hibel

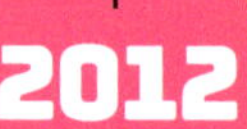

Jeremy Boyle & Kevin Clancy .... Syncopated Rhythm

John Peña .... Things That Fly

Jonathan Armistead & Scott Andrew .... Kitty Kiddie Meow Meow

Will Schlough .... Barrels!

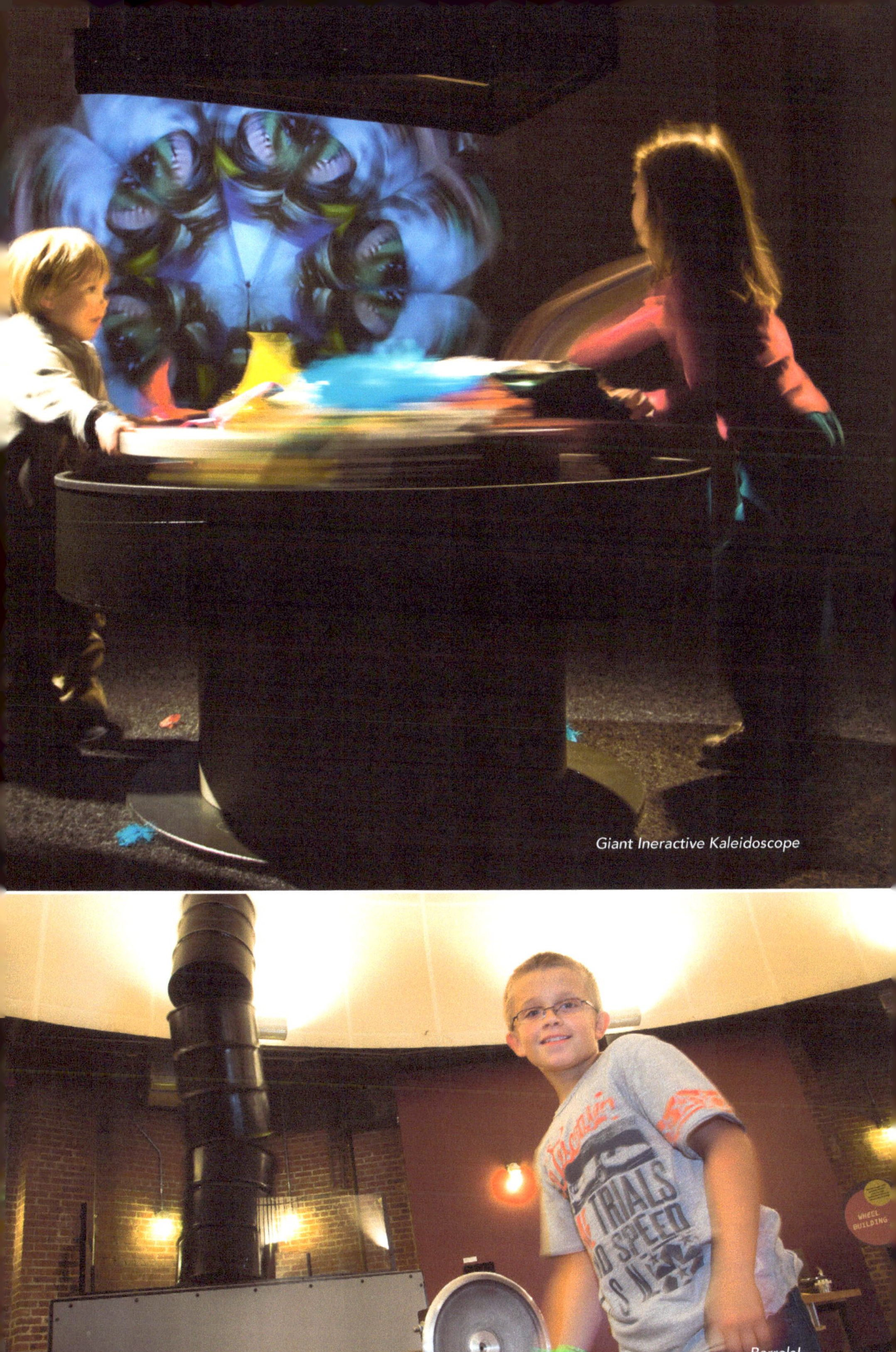

Giant Ineractive Kaleidoscope

Barrels!

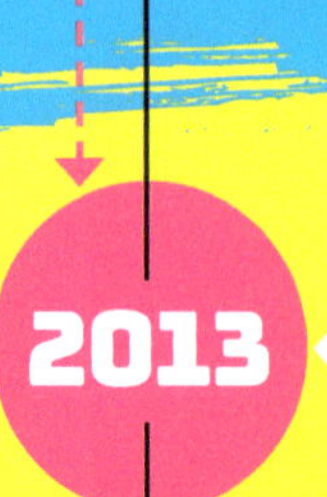

2013

Chris Beauregard	Pyramids
Isla Hansen & Luke Loeffler	Monstroscopy
Katie Ford	Fragment Field
Scott Garner	Reach

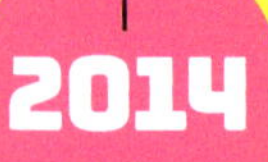

2014

Dakotah Konicek & Jesse Kauppila	Fissure and Quake
Jenna Boyles	Space Sheep
Lindsay Packer	Prism Palace
Stephanie Ross	OmniNimbus

2015

Ann Tarantino	Moon, Shine
Charles Sowers	Shy Lights
Danny Bracken	Feeeedbaaaaak
Rachel Buse	Giant Breath Taker

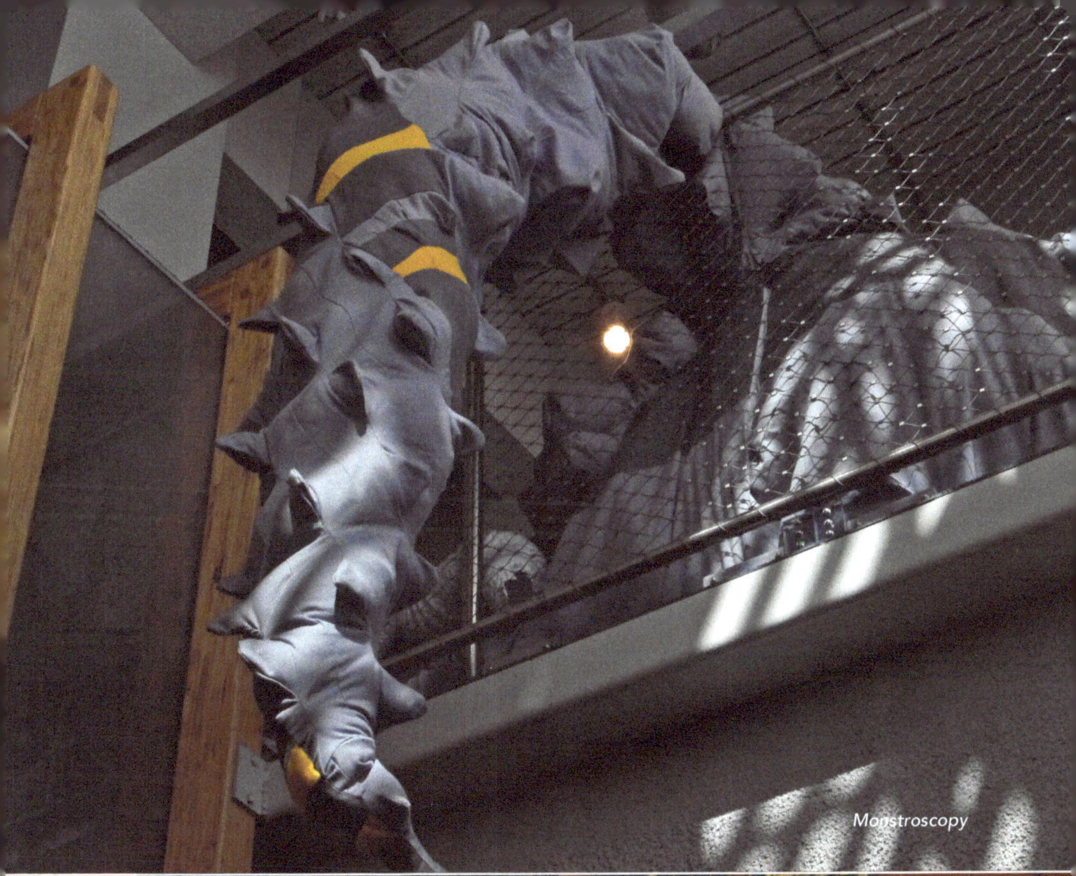

Monstroscopy

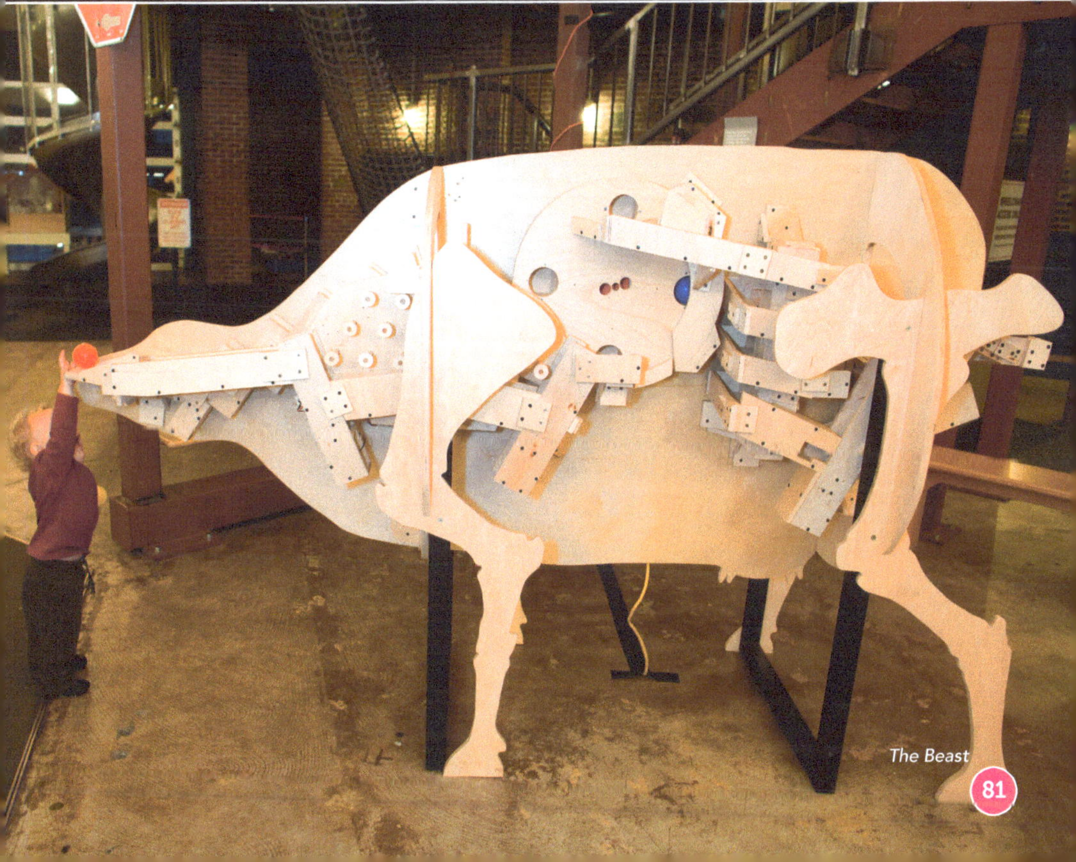

The Beast

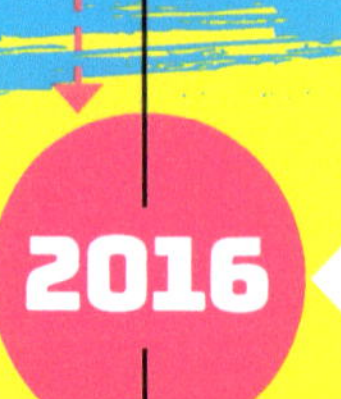

2016

Anne Lilly .... To Conjugate

Nicholas Hanna .... Bubble Device #5

Nobuho Nagasawa .... Fist Sized Survival

Stephen Malinowski ... Music Animation Machine

2017

H. Gene Thompson & Arvid Tomayko .... Urchin Searchin Sound

Megan Flød Johnson ... The NEST

Robert Zacharias .... Drawn Together

Shohei Katayama .... Nimbus Drum

2018

Isaac Levine .... Lake Light

Lumi Barron & Miranda Miller .... Light Showers

Neil Mendoza .... Mechanical Masterpieces

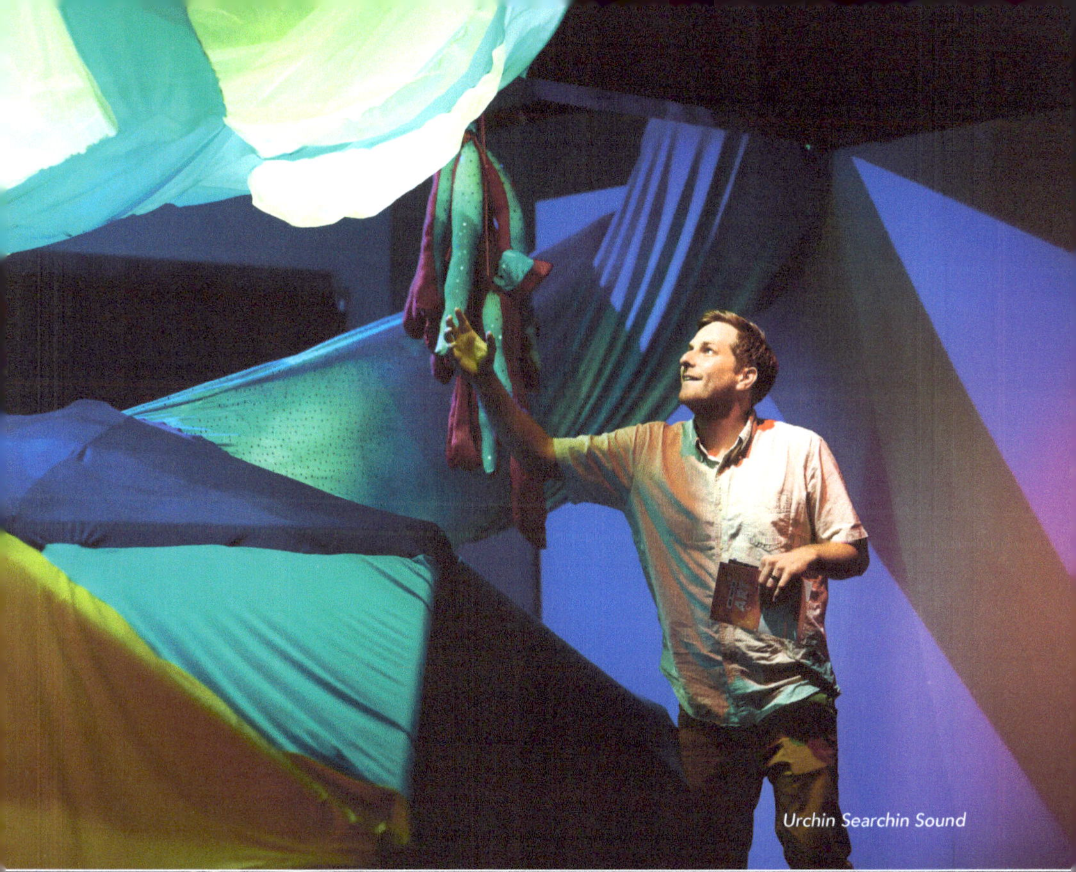

Urchin Searchin Sound

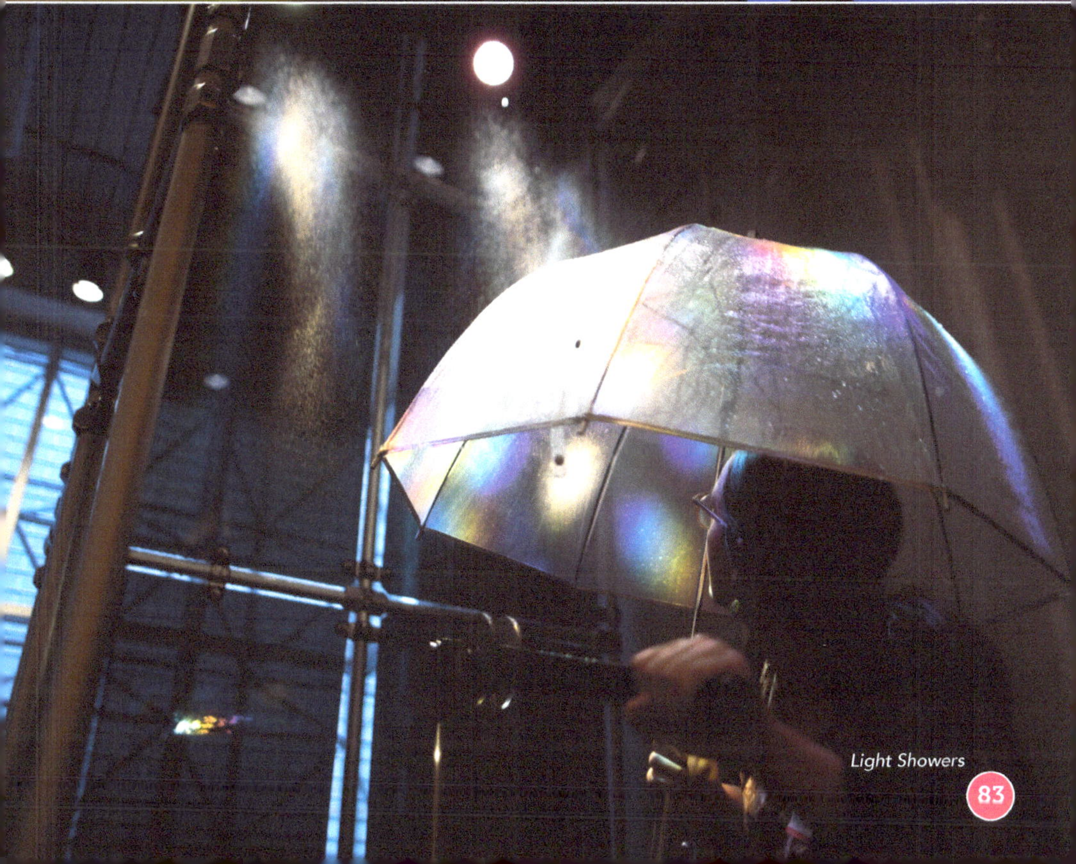

Light Showers

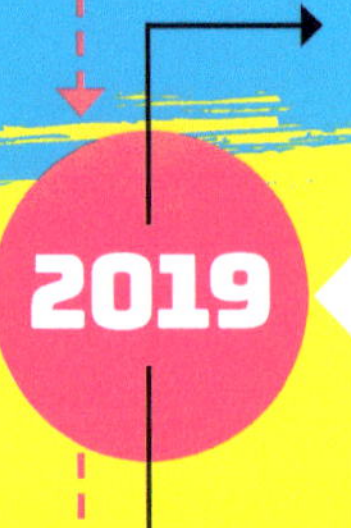

2019

Eunice Choi .... Tomato Medley

Owen Lowery .... Cosmic Geometry

Ryder Henry .... Compound Ringship

2020 @Home

Anna Garner .... Camera Constructions

Brooke Barker .... Make Your Own Sad Animal Fact

Ibiyinka Alao .... Painting Light

Jeff Repko .... Marvelous Machines

Suwan Kim .... Pop-Up Shadow Puppet Theatre

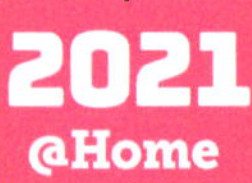

2021 @Home

Karl Lorenzen .... Patterns of Beauty

Lauren Braun .... Create Your Own Paper Cutout Artwork

Maria Fox Larsson ... How to Build a Wire Creature

Nikita Zook .... Make an Abstract Collage

Sidney Mullis .... Create Your Own Make-Believe Forest

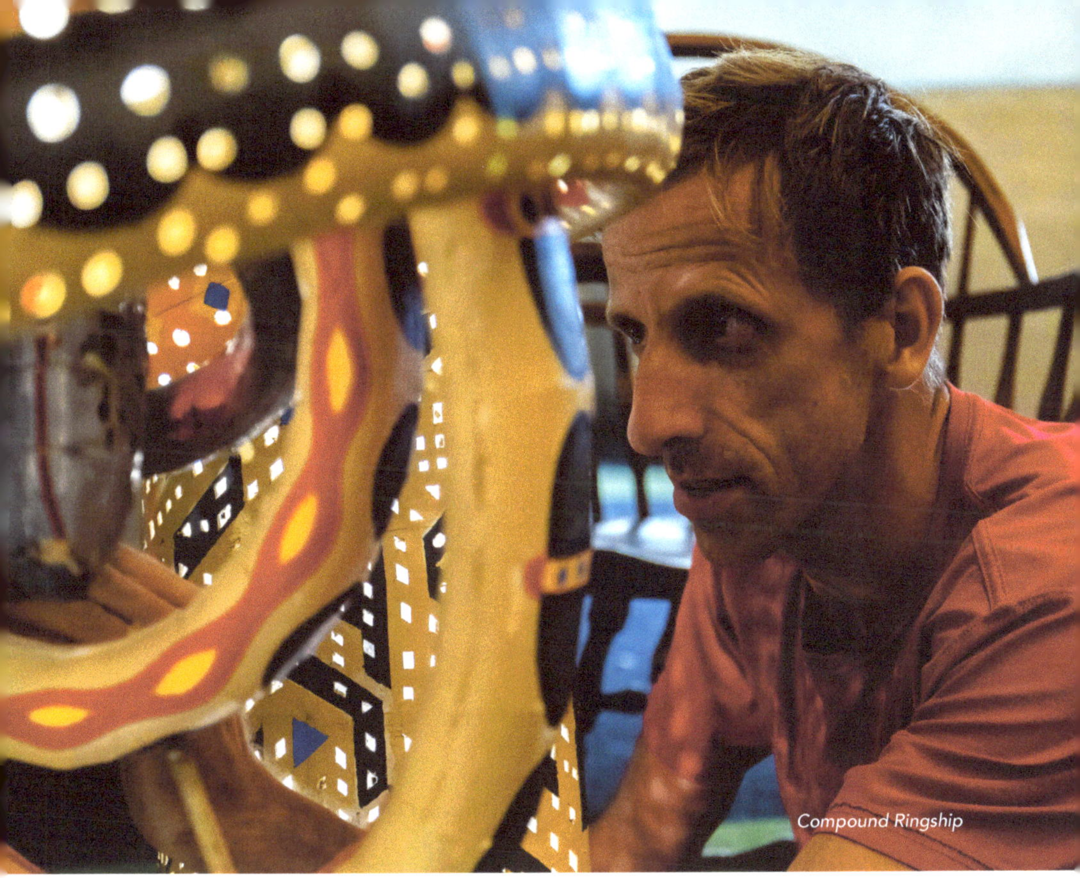

Compound Ringship

AKING YOUR OWN SAD ANIMAL FACT WITH BROOKE BARKER

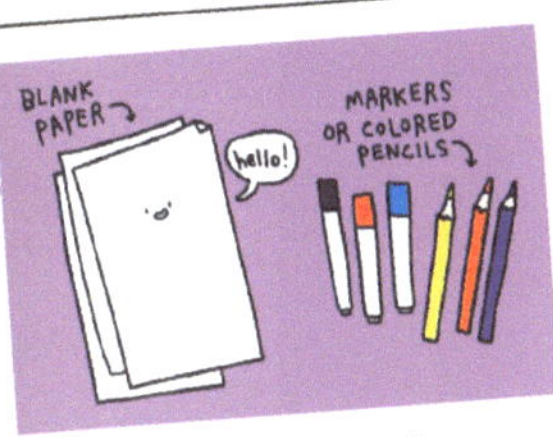

1) First, gather your supplies.

2) Choose an animal fact you'd like to illustrate. You can use a book or nature program for inspiration, write a fact about your pet, or use one of these:

BLOBFISH HAVE NO MUSCLES

BEES HAVE HAIR ON THEIR EYES

FOXES LIVE ALONE

AN OPOSSUM MOM CARRIES HER BABIES ON HER BACK

OWLS HAVE EYETUBES INSTEAD OF EYEBALLS

HORSES CAN SLEEP STANDING UP

SOME LIZARDS USE PUSH-UPS TO SAY HI

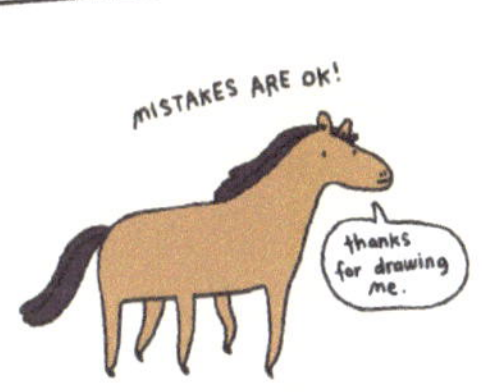

3) I like to draw in pen and make any mistakes a part of my drawing. Mistakes make your drawing unique, and they give your animal more personality. And if your animal drawing has extra long legs or a different kind of ears, or wiggly stripes -- you just invented a new animal.

4) Animals can be covered in fur, feathers, scales, spikes, spots, or stripes, but you don't need to draw every single one. Instead you can just draw a few of them. Usually I draw them in groups of two or three.

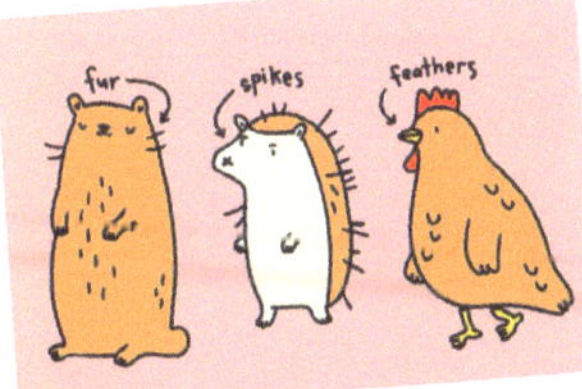

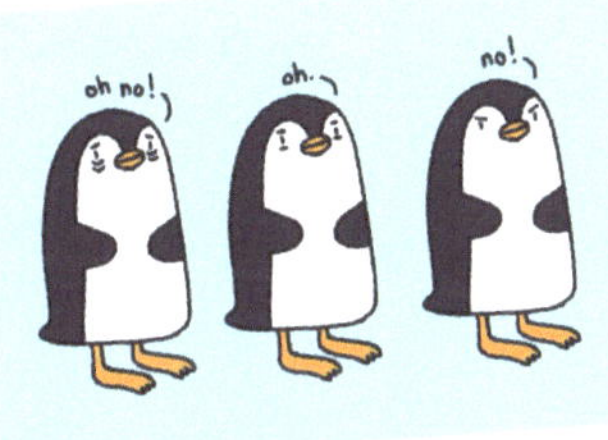

5) Eyebrows can change a drawing's mood, just ask this penguin.

6) The secret to drawing speech bubbles Is to write the words first! After you've written the words, draw the speech bubble around them.

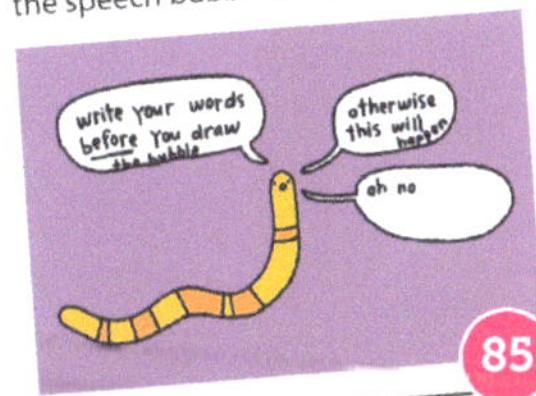

INDEX

Image Credits

Armistead, Jonathan / Andrew, Scott: 30–32
Boyles, Jenna: 50–52
Butts, David: 17 (background), 19–20
Choi, Eunice: 64 (top)
Garner, Scott: 40 (top), 41 (top), 42 (bottom)
Hoover, Kristi Jan ©: 4, 10, 34, 37, 43 (top), 44, 46, 47, 49, 81 (bottom), 87
Kiger, Rebecca ©: 88
Packer, Lindsay: 26
Rosensteel, Renee ©: 81

Index of Names

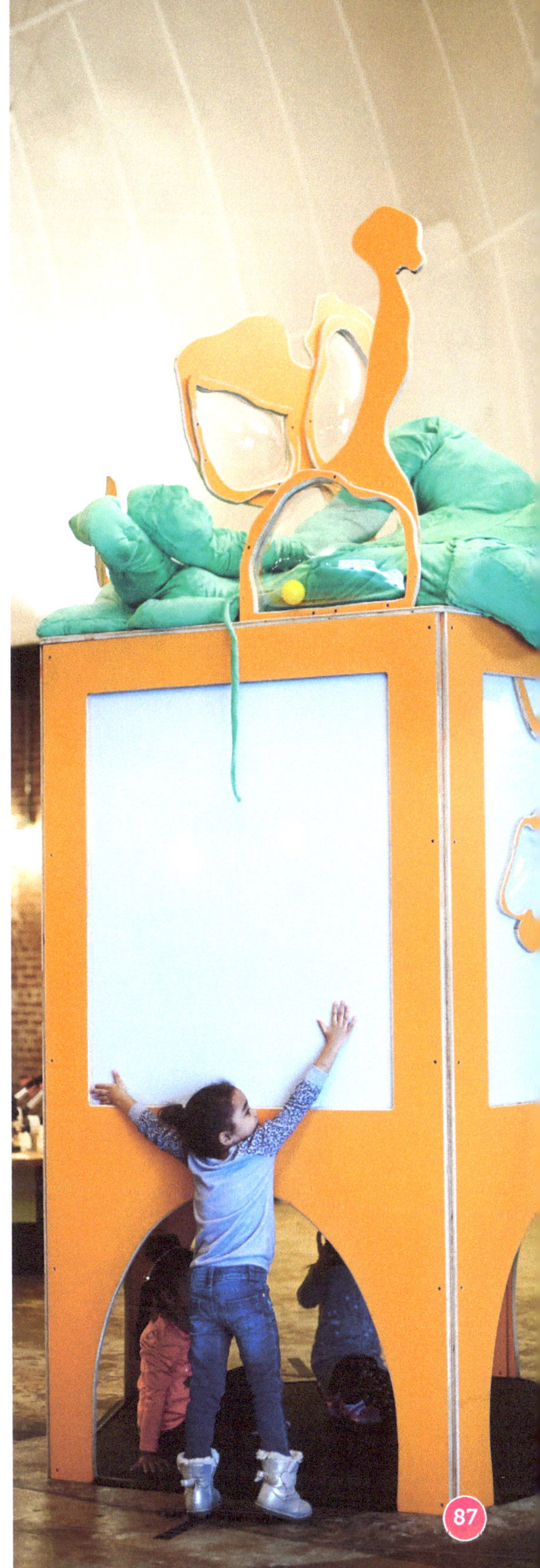

Right: *Giant Breath Taker* (Rachel Buse 2015)

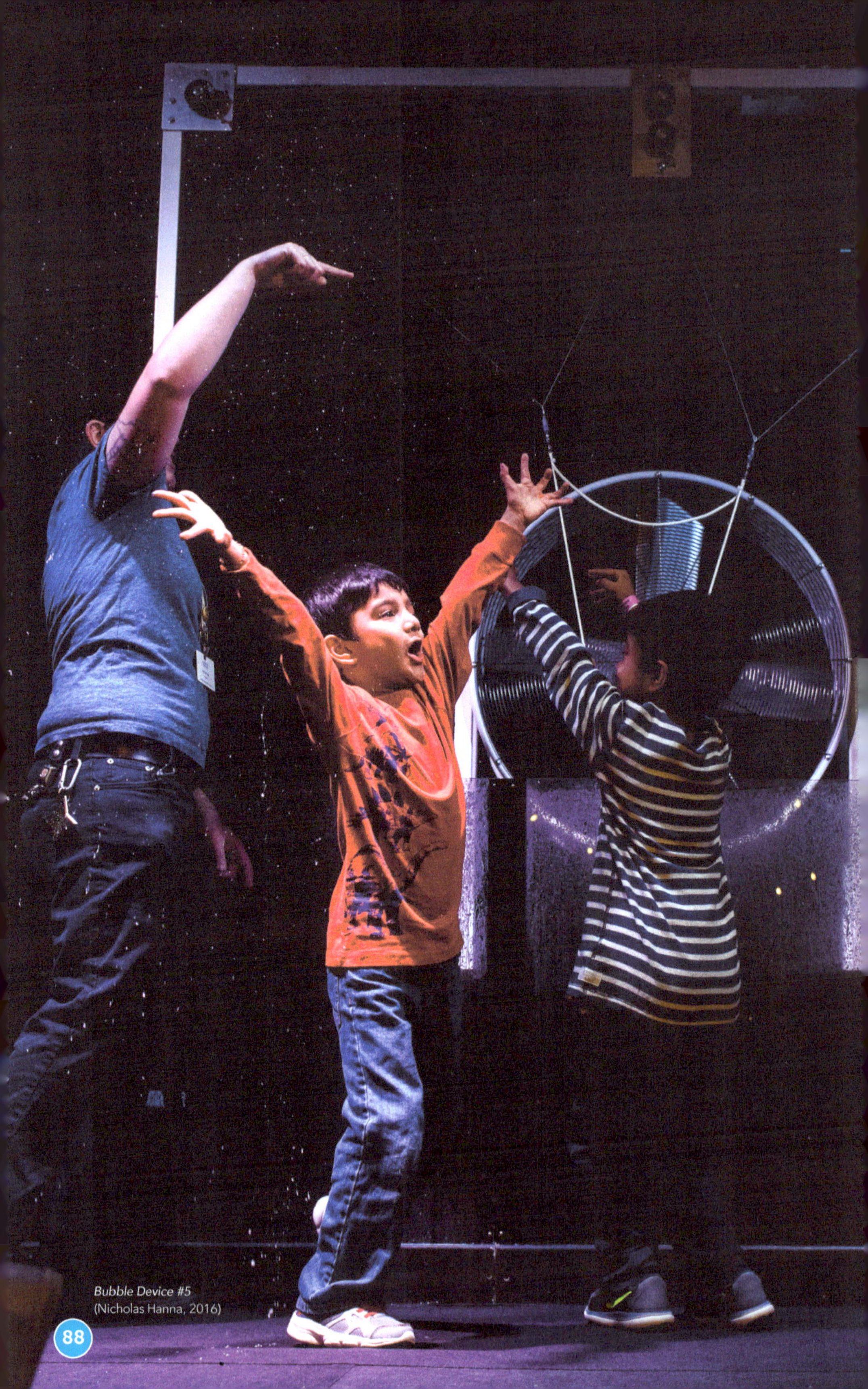

Bubble Device #5
(Nicholas Hanna, 2016)